CS-69   GENERAL APTITUDE AND ABILITIES SERIES

This is your
PASSBOOK for...

Evaluating Conclusions in Light of Known Facts

Test Preparation Study Guide
Questions & Answers

NATIONAL LEARNING CORPORATION®

COPYRIGHT NOTICE

This book is SOLELY intended for, is sold ONLY to, and its use is RESTRICTED to individual, bona fide applicants or candidates who qualify by virtue of having seriously filed applications for appropriate license, certificate, professional and/or promotional advancement, higher school matriculation, scholarship, or other legitimate requirements of education and/or governmental authorities.

This book is NOT intended for use, class instruction, tutoring, training, duplication, copying, reprinting, excerption, or adaptation, etc., by:

1) Other publishers
2) Proprietors and/or Instructors of "Coaching" and/or Preparatory Courses
3) Personnel and/or Training Divisions of commercial, industrial, and governmental organizations
4) Schools, colleges, or universities and/or their departments and staffs, including teachers and other personnel
5) Testing Agencies or Bureaus
6) Study groups which seek by the purchase of a single volume to copy and/or duplicate and/or adapt this material for use by the group as a whole without having purchased individual volumes for each of the members of the group
7) Et al.

Such persons would be in violation of appropriate Federal and State statutes.

PROVISION OF LICENSING AGREEMENTS – Recognized educational, commercial, industrial, and governmental institutions and organizations, and others legitimately engaged in educational pursuits, including training, testing, and measurement activities, may address request for a licensing agreement to the copyright owners, who will determine whether, and under what conditions, including fees and charges, the materials in this book may be used them. In other words, a licensing facility exists for the legitimate use of the material in this book on other than an individual basis. However, it is asseverated and affirmed here that the material in this book CANNOT be used without the receipt of the express permission of such a licensing agreement from the Publishers. Inquiries re licensing should be addressed to the company, attention rights and permissions department.

All rights reserved, including the right of reproduction in whole or in part, in any form or by any means, electronic or mechanical, including photocopying, recording, or by any information storage and retrieval system, without permission in writing from the Publisher.

Copyright © 2024 by
National Learning Corporation

212 Michael Drive, Syosset, NY 11791
(516) 921-8888 • www.passbooks.com
E-mail: info@passbooks.com

PUBLISHED IN THE UNITED STATES OF AMERICA

PASSBOOK® SERIES

THE *PASSBOOK® SERIES* has been created to prepare applicants and candidates for the ultimate academic battlefield – the examination room.

At some time in our lives, each and every one of us may be required to take an examination – for validation, matriculation, admission, qualification, registration, certification, or licensure.

Based on the assumption that every applicant or candidate has met the basic formal educational standards, has taken the required number of courses, and read the necessary texts, the *PASSBOOK® SERIES* furnishes the one special preparation which may assure passing with confidence, instead of failing with insecurity. Examination questions – together with answers – are furnished as the basic vehicle for study so that the mysteries of the examination and its compounding difficulties may be eliminated or diminished by a sure method.

This book is meant to help you pass your examination provided that you qualify and are serious in your objective.

The entire field is reviewed through the huge store of content information which is succinctly presented through a provocative and challenging approach – the question-and-answer method.

A climate of success is established by furnishing the correct answers at the end of each test.

You soon learn to recognize types of questions, forms of questions, and patterns of questioning. You may even begin to anticipate expected outcomes.

You perceive that many questions are repeated or adapted so that you can gain acute insights, which may enable you to score many sure points.

You learn how to confront new questions, or types of questions, and to attack them confidently and work out the correct answers.

You note objectives and emphases, and recognize pitfalls and dangers, so that you may make positive educational adjustments.

Moreover, you are kept fully informed in relation to new concepts, methods, practices, and directions in the field.

You discover that you are actually taking the examination all the time: you are preparing for the examination by "taking" an examination, not by reading extraneous and/or supererogatory textbooks.

In short, this PASSBOOK®, used directedly, should be an important factor in helping you to pass your test.

EVALUATING CONCLUSIONS BASED ON FACTUAL INFORMATION

Test material will be presented in a multiple-choice question format.

Test Task: You will be given a set of statements and a conclusion based on the statements. You are to assume the statements are true. The conclusion is reached from these statements *only-not* on what you may happen to know about the subject discussed. Each question has three possible answers. You must then select the correct answer in the following manner:

Select A, if the statements prove that the conclusion is true.
Select B, if the statements prove that the conclusion is false.
Select C, if the statements are inadequate to prove the conclusion either true or false.

SAMPLE QUESTION #1:

STATEMENTS: All uniforms are cleaned by the Conroy Company. Blue uniforms are cleaned on Mondays or Fridays; green or brown uniforms are cleaned on Wednesdays. Alan and Jean have blue uniforms, Gary has green uniforms and Ryan has brown uniforms.

CONCLUSION: Jean's uniforms are cleaned on Wednesdays.
  A. statements prove the conclusion TRUE
  B. statements prove the conclusion FALSE
  C. statements are INADEQUATE to prove the conclusion

The correct answer to this sample question is Choice B.

Solution:

The last sentence of the statements says that jean has blue uniforms. the second sentence of the statements says that blue uniforms are cleaned on Monday or Friday.
the conclusion says jean's uniforms are cleaned on Wednesday. Wednesday is neither Monday or Friday. Therefore, the conclusion must be false (choice B).

SAMPLE QUESTION #2:

STATEMENTS: If Beth works overtime, the assignment will be completed. If the assignment is completed, then all unit employees will receive a bonus. Beth works overtime.

CONCLUSION: A bonus will be given to all employees in the unit.
   A. statement prove the conclusion TRUE
   B. statements prove the conclusion FALSE
   C. statements are INADEQUATE to prove the conclusion

The correct answer to this sample question is Choice A.

Solution:

The conclusion follows necessarily from the statements. Beth works overtime. The assignment is completed. Therefore, all unit employees will receive a bonus.

SAMPLE QUESTION #3:

STATEMENTS: Bill is older than Wanda. Edna is older than Bill. Sarah is twice as old as Wanda.

CONCLUSION: Sarah is older than Edna.

   A. statement prove the conclusion TRUE
   B. statements prove the conclusion FALSE
   C. statements are INADEQUATE to prove the conclusion

The correct answer to this sample question is Choice C.

Solution:

We know from the statements that both Sarah and Edna are older than Wanda. We do not have any other information about Sarah and Edna. Therefore, no conclusion about whether or not Sarah is older than Edna can be made.

EVALUATING CONCLUSIONS IN LIGHT OF KNOWN FACTS

An ability needed in many state jobs is the ability to decide if a conclusion is true, based on a set of facts. (These questions can also be called "Logic".) First read the facts (or premises) that are given, and then look at the conclusion. Assume the facts are true, and decide if the conclusion is:

1. Necessarily true.
2. Probably, but not necessarily true.
3. Indeterminable, cannot be determined.
4. Probably, but not necessarily false.
5. Necessarily false.

These five answer choices (above) are the same for each inference question.

1. FACTS: If the Commission approves the new proposal, the agency will move to a new location immediately. If the agency moves, five new supervisors will be appointed immediately. The Commission approved the new proposal.

    CONCLUSION: No new supervisors were appointed.

    1. Necessarily true.
    2. Probably, but not necessarily true.
    3. Indeterminable, cannot be determined.
    4. Probably, but not necessarily false.
    5. Necessarily false.

2. FACTS: If the director retires, John Jackson, the associate director, will not be transferred to another agency. Jackson will be promoted to director if he is not transferred. The director retired.

    CONCLUSION: Jackson will be promoted to director.

    1. Necessarily true.
    2. Probably, but not necessarily true.
    3. Indeterminable, cannot be determined.
    4. Probably, but not necessarily false.
    5. Necessarily false.

3. **FACTS:** If the maximum allowable income for food stamp recipients is increased, the number of food stamp recipients will increase. If the number of food stamp recipients increases, more funds must be allocated to the food stamp program, which will require a tax increase. Taxes cannot be raised without the approval of Congress. Congress probably will not approve a tax increase.

   CONCLUSION: The maximum allowable income for food stamp recipients will increase.

   1. Necessarily true.
   2. Probably, but not necessarily true.
   3. Indeterminable, cannot be determined.
   4. Probably, but not necessarily false.
   5. Necessarily false.

4. **FACTS:** If prices are raised and sales remain constant, profits will increase. Prices were raised and sales levels will probably be maintained.

   CONCLUSION: Profits will increase.

   1. Necessarily true.
   2. Probably, but not necessarily true.
   3. Indeterminable, cannot be determined.
   4. Probably, but not necessarily false.
   5. Necessarily false.

5. **FACTS:** Some employees in the personnel department are technicians. Most of the technicians working in the personnel department are test development specialists. Lisa Jones works in the personnel department.

   CONCLUSION: Lisa Jones is a technician.

   1. Necessarily true.
   2. Probably, but not necessarily true.
   3. Indeterminable, cannot be determined.
   4. Probably, but not necessarily false.
   5. Necessarily false.

INFERENCE QUESTION ANSWERS AND EXPLANATIONS

1. The correct answer is number 5 (necessarily false). The new proposal was approved. According to the facts, approval means that the agency will move, and moving to a new location means that five new supervisors will be appointed.

2. The correct answer is number 1 (necessarily true). According to the facts, the director retired, which means that Jackson will not be transferred and, therefore, will be promoted to director.

3. The correct answer is number 4 (probably, but not necessarily false). Since Congress probably will not approve a tax increase, the maximum allowable income for food stamp recipients probably will not increase.

4. The correct answer is number 2 (probably, but not necessarily true). According to the facts, profits will increase if prices are raised and sales remain constant. It is known that prices were raised. Although sales level will probably be maintained, this is not certain.

5. The correct answer is number 3 (indeterminable, cannot be determined). The facts give no indication of the proportion of employees who are technicians. Therefore, no conclusion can be drawn with respect to the probability that any one employee is a technician.

HOW TO TAKE A TEST

You have studied long, hard and conscientiously.

With your official admission card in hand, and your heart pounding, you have been admitted to the examination room.

You note that there are several hundred other applicants in the examination room waiting to take the same test.

They all appear to be equally well prepared.

You know that nothing but your best effort will suffice. The "moment of truth" is at hand: you now have to demonstrate objectively, in writing, your knowledge of content and your understanding of subject matter.

You are fighting the most important battle of your life—to pass and/or score high on an examination which will determine your career and provide the economic basis for your livelihood.

What extra, special things should you know and should you do in taking the examination?

I. YOU MUST PASS AN EXAMINATION

A. WHAT EVERY CANDIDATE SHOULD KNOW
Examination applicants often ask us for help in preparing for the written test. What can I study in advance? What kinds of questions will be asked? How will the test be given? How will the papers be graded?

B. HOW ARE EXAMS DEVELOPED?
Examinations are carefully written by trained technicians who are specialists in the field known as "psychological measurement," in consultation with recognized authorities in the field of work that the test will cover. These experts recommend the subject matter areas or skills to be tested; only those knowledges or skills important to your success on the job are included. The most reliable books and source materials available are used as references. Together, the experts and technicians judge the difficulty level of the questions.
Test technicians know how to phrase questions so that the problem is clearly stated. Their ethics do not permit "trick" or "catch" questions. Questions may have been tried out on sample groups, or subjected to statistical analysis, to determine their usefulness.
Written tests are often used in combination with performance tests, ratings of training and experience, and oral interviews. All of these measures combine to form the best-known means of finding the right person for the right job.

II. HOW TO PASS THE WRITTEN TEST

A. BASIC STEPS

1) Study the announcement

How, then, can you know what subjects to study? Our best answer is: "Learn as much as possible about the class of positions for which you've applied." The exam will test the knowledge, skills and abilities needed to do the work.

Your most valuable source of information about the position you want is the official exam announcement. This announcement lists the training and experience qualifications. Check these standards and apply only if you come reasonably close to meeting them. Many jurisdictions preview the written test in the exam announcement by including a section called "Knowledge and Abilities Required," "Scope of the Examination," or some similar heading. Here you will find out specifically what fields will be tested.

2) Choose appropriate study materials

If the position for which you are applying is technical or advanced, you will read more advanced, specialized material. If you are already familiar with the basic principles of your field, elementary textbooks would waste your time. Concentrate on advanced textbooks and technical periodicals. Think through the concepts and review difficult problems in your field.

These are all general sources. You can get more ideas on your own initiative, following these leads. For example, training manuals and publications of the government agency which employs workers in your field can be useful, particularly for technical and professional positions. A letter or visit to the government department involved may result in more specific study suggestions, and certainly will provide you with a more definite idea of the exact nature of the position you are seeking.

3) Study this book!

III. KINDS OF TESTS

Tests are used for purposes other than measuring knowledge and ability to perform specified duties. For some positions, it is equally important to test ability to make adjustments to new situations or to profit from training. In others, basic mental abilities not dependent on information are essential. Questions which test these things may not appear as pertinent to the duties of the position as those which test for knowledge and information. Yet they are often highly important parts of a fair examination. For very general questions, it is almost impossible to help you direct your study efforts. What we can do is to point out some of the more common of these general abilities needed in public service positions and describe some typical questions.

1) General information

Broad, general information has been found useful for predicting job success in some kinds of work. This is tested in a variety of ways, from vocabulary lists to questions about current events. Basic background in some field of work, such as sociology or economics, may be sampled in a group of questions. Often these are principles which have become familiar to most persons through exposure rather than through formal training. It is difficult to advise you how to study for these questions; being alert to the world around you is our best suggestion.

2) Verbal ability

An example of an ability needed in many positions is verbal or language ability. Verbal ability is, in brief, the ability to use and understand words. Vocabulary and grammar tests are typical measures of this ability. Reading comprehension or paragraph interpretation questions are common in many kinds of civil service tests. You are given a paragraph of written material and asked to find its central meaning.

IV. KINDS OF QUESTIONS

1. Multiple-choice Questions

Most popular of the short-answer questions is the "multiple choice" or "best answer" question. It can be used, for example, to test for factual knowledge, ability to solve problems or judgment in meeting situations found at work.

A multiple-choice question is normally one of three types:
- It can begin with an incomplete statement followed by several possible endings. You are to find the one ending which best completes the statement, although some of the others may not be entirely wrong.
- It can also be a complete statement in the form of a question which is answered by choosing one of the statements listed.
- It can be in the form of a problem – again you select the best answer.

Here is an example of a multiple-choice question with a discussion which should give you some clues as to the method for choosing the right answer:

When an employee has a complaint about his assignment, the action which will best help him overcome his difficulty is to
    A. discuss his difficulty with his coworkers
    B. take the problem to the head of the organization
    C. take the problem to the person who gave him the assignment
    D. say nothing to anyone about his complaint

In answering this question, you should study each of the choices to find which is best. Consider choice "A" – Certainly an employee may discuss his complaint with fellow employees, but no change or improvement can result, and the complaint remains unresolved. Choice "B" is a poor choice since the head of the organization probably does not know what assignment you have been given, and taking your problem to him is known as "going over the head" of the supervisor. The supervisor, or person who made the assignment, is the person who can clarify it or correct any injustice. Choice "C" is, therefore, correct. To say nothing, as in choice "D," is unwise. Supervisors have and interest in knowing the problems employees are facing, and the employee is seeking a solution to his problem.

2. True/False

3. Matching Questions

Matching an answer from a column of choices within another column.

V. RECORDING YOUR ANSWERS

Computer terminals are used more and more today for many different kinds of exams.

For an examination with very few applicants, you may be told to record your answers in the test booklet itself. Separate answer sheets are much more common. If this separate answer sheet is to be scored by machine – and this is often the case – it is highly important that you mark your answers correctly in order to get credit.

VI. BEFORE THE TEST

YOUR PHYSICAL CONDITION IS IMPORTANT

If you are not well, you can't do your best work on tests. If you are half asleep, you can't do your best either. Here are some tips:

1) Get about the same amount of sleep you usually get. Don't stay up all night before the test, either partying or worrying—DON'T DO IT!
2) If you wear glasses, be sure to wear them when you go to take the test. This goes for hearing aids, too.
3) If you have any physical problems that may keep you from doing your best, be sure to tell the person giving the test. If you are sick or in poor health, you relay cannot do your best on any test. You can always come back and take the test some other time.

Common sense will help you find procedures to follow to get ready for an examination. Too many of us, however, overlook these sensible measures. Indeed, nervousness and fatigue have been found to be the most serious reasons why applicants fail to do their best on civil service tests. Here is a list of reminders:

- Begin your preparation early – Don't wait until the last minute to go scurrying around for books and materials or to find out what the position is all about.
- Prepare continuously – An hour a night for a week is better than an all-night cram session. This has been definitely established. What is more, a night a week for a month will return better dividends than crowding your study into a shorter period of time.
- Locate the place of the exam – You have been sent a notice telling you when and where to report for the examination. If the location is in a different town or otherwise unfamiliar to you, it would be well to inquire the best route and learn something about the building.
- Relax the night before the test – Allow your mind to rest. Do not study at all that night. Plan some mild recreation or diversion; then go to bed early and get a good night's sleep.
- Get up early enough to make a leisurely trip to the place for the test – This way unforeseen events, traffic snarls, unfamiliar buildings, etc. will not upset you.
- Dress comfortably – A written test is not a fashion show. You will be known by number and not by name, so wear something comfortable.
- Leave excess paraphernalia at home – Shopping bags and odd bundles will get in your way. You need bring only the items mentioned in the official notice you received; usually everything you need is provided. Do not bring reference books to the exam. They will only confuse those last minutes and be taken away from you when in the test room.

- Arrive somewhat ahead of time – If because of transportation schedules you must get there very early, bring a newspaper or magazine to take your mind off yourself while waiting.
- Locate the examination room – When you have found the proper room, you will be directed to the seat or part of the room where you will sit. Sometimes you are given a sheet of instructions to read while you are waiting. Do not fill out any forms until you are told to do so; just read them and be prepared.
- Relax and prepare to listen to the instructions
- If you have any physical problem that may keep you from doing your best, be sure to tell the test administrator. If you are sick or in poor health, you really cannot do your best on the exam. You can come back and take the test some other time.

VII. AT THE TEST

The day of the test is here and you have the test booklet in your hand. The temptation to get going is very strong. Caution! There is more to success than knowing the right answers. You must know how to identify your papers and understand variations in the type of short-answer question used in this particular examination. Follow these suggestions for maximum results from your efforts:

1) Cooperate with the monitor

The test administrator has a duty to create a situation in which you can be as much at ease as possible. He will give instructions, tell you when to begin, check to see that you are marking your answer sheet correctly, and so on. He is not there to guard you, although he will see that your competitors do not take unfair advantage. He wants to help you do your best.

2) Listen to all instructions

Don't jump the gun! Wait until you understand all directions. In most civil service tests you get more time than you need to answer the questions. So don't be in a hurry. Read each word of instructions until you clearly understand the meaning. Study the examples, listen to all announcements and follow directions. Ask questions if you do not understand what to do.

3) Identify your papers

Civil service exams are usually identified by number only. You will be assigned a number; you must not put your name on your test papers. Be sure to copy your number correctly. Since more than one exam may be given, copy your exact examination title.

4) Plan your time

Unless you are told that a test is a "speed" or "rate of work" test, speed itself is usually not important. Time enough to answer all the questions will be provided, but this does not mean that you have all day. An overall time limit has been set. Divide the total time (in minutes) by the number of questions to determine the approximate time you have for each question.

5) Do not linger over difficult questions

If you come across a difficult question, mark it with a paper clip (useful to have along) and come back to it when you have been through the booklet. One caution if you do this – be sure to skip a number on your answer sheet as well. Check often to be sure that you have not lost your place and that you are marking in the row numbered the same as the question you are answering.

6) Read the questions
   Be sure you know what the question asks! Many capable people are unsuccessful because they failed to read the questions correctly.

7) Answer all questions
   Unless you have been instructed that a penalty will be deducted for incorrect answers, it is better to guess than to omit a question.

8) Speed tests
   It is often better NOT to guess on speed tests. It has been found that on timed tests people are tempted to spend the last few seconds before time is called in marking answers at random – without even reading them – in the hope of picking up a few extra points. To discourage this practice, the instructions may warn you that your score will be "corrected" for guessing. That is, a penalty will be applied. The incorrect answers will be deducted from the correct ones, or some other penalty formula will be used.

9) Review your answers
   If you finish before time is called, go back to the questions you guessed or omitted to give them further thought. Review other answers if you have time.

10) Return your test materials
    If you are ready to leave before others have finished or time is called, take ALL your materials to the monitor and leave quietly. Never take any test material with you. The monitor can discover whose papers are not complete, and taking a test booklet may be grounds for disqualification.

VIII. EXAMINATION TECHNIQUES

1) Read the general instructions carefully. These are usually printed on the first page of the exam booklet. As a rule, these instructions refer to the timing of the examination; the fact that you should not start work until the signal and must stop work at a signal, etc. If there are any special instructions, such as a choice of questions to be answered, make sure that you note this instruction carefully.

2) When you are ready to start work on the examination, that is as soon as the signal has been given, read the instructions to each question booklet, underline any key words or phrases, such as least, best, outline, describe and the like. In this way you will tend to answer as requested rather than discover on reviewing your paper that you listed without describing, that you selected the worst choice rather than the best choice, etc.

3) If the examination is of the objective or multiple-choice type – that is, each question will also give a series of possible answers: A, B, C or D, and you are called upon to select the best answer and write the letter next to that answer on your answer paper – it is advisable to start answering each question in turn. There may be anywhere from 50 to 100 such questions in the three or four hours allotted and you can see how much time would be taken if you read through all the questions before beginning to answer any. Furthermore, if you

come across a question or group of questions which you know would be difficult to answer, it would undoubtedly affect your handling of all the other questions.

4) If the examination is of the essay type and contains but a few questions, it is a moot point as to whether you should read all the questions before starting to answer any one. Of course, if you are given a choice – say five out of seven and the like – then it is essential to read all the questions so you can eliminate the two that are most difficult. If, however, you are asked to answer all the questions, there may be danger in trying to answer the easiest one first because you may find that you will spend too much time on it. The best technique is to answer the first question, then proceed to the second, etc.

5) Time your answers. Before the exam begins, write down the time it started, then add the time allowed for the examination and write down the time it must be completed, then divide the time available somewhat as follows:
   - If 3-1/2 hours are allowed, that would be 210 minutes. If you have 80 objective-type questions, that would be an average of 2-1/2 minutes per question. Allow yourself no more than 2 minutes per question, or a total of 160 minutes, which will permit about 50 minutes to review.
   - If for the time allotment of 210 minutes there are 7 essay questions to answer, that would average about 30 minutes a question. Give yourself only 25 minutes per question so that you have about 35 minutes to review.

6) The most important instruction is to read each question and make sure you know what is wanted. The second most important instruction is to time yourself properly so that you answer every question. The third most important instruction is to answer every question. Guess if you have to but include something for each question. Remember that you will receive no credit for a blank and will probably receive some credit if you write something in answer to an essay question. If you guess a letter – say "B" for a multiple-choice question – you may have guessed right. If you leave a blank as an answer to a multiple-choice question, the examiners may respect your feelings but it will not add a point to your score. Some exams may penalize you for wrong answers, so in such cases only, you may not want to guess unless you have some basis for your answer.

7) Suggestions
   a. Objective-type questions
      1. Examine the question booklet for proper sequence of pages and questions
      2. Read all instructions carefully
      3. Skip any question which seems too difficult; return to it after all other questions have been answered
      4. Apportion your time properly; do not spend too much time on any single question or group of questions
      5. Note and underline key words – all, most, fewest, least, best, worst, same, opposite, etc.
      6. Pay particular attention to negatives
      7. Note unusual option, e.g., unduly long, short, complex, different or similar in content to the body of the question
      8. Observe the use of "hedging" words – probably, may, most likely, etc.

9. Make sure that your answer is put next to the same number as the question
10. Do not second-guess unless you have good reason to believe the second answer is definitely more correct
11. Cross out original answer if you decide another answer is more accurate; do not erase until you are ready to hand your paper in
12. Answer all questions; guess unless instructed otherwise
13. Leave time for review

b. Essay questions
1. Read each question carefully
2. Determine exactly what is wanted. Underline key words or phrases.
3. Decide on outline or paragraph answer
4. Include many different points and elements unless asked to develop any one or two points or elements
5. Show impartiality by giving pros and cons unless directed to select one side only
6. Make and write down any assumptions you find necessary to answer the questions
7. Watch your English, grammar, punctuation and choice of words
8. Time your answers; don't crowd material

8) Answering the essay question

Most essay questions can be answered by framing the specific response around several key words or ideas. Here are a few such key words or ideas:

M's: manpower, materials, methods, money, management
P's: purpose, program, policy, plan, procedure, practice, problems, pitfalls, personnel, public relations

a. Six basic steps in handling problems:
1. Preliminary plan and background development
2. Collect information, data and facts
3. Analyze and interpret information, data and facts
4. Analyze and develop solutions as well as make recommendations
5. Prepare report and sell recommendations
6. Install recommendations and follow up effectiveness

b. Pitfalls to avoid
1. Taking things for granted – A statement of the situation does not necessarily imply that each of the elements is necessarily true; for example, a complaint may be invalid and biased so that all that can be taken for granted is that a complaint has been registered
2. Considering only one side of a situation – Wherever possible, indicate several alternatives and then point out the reasons you selected the best one
3. Failing to indicate follow up – Whenever your answer indicates action on your part, make certain that you will take proper follow-up action to see how successful your recommendations, procedures or actions turn out to be
4. Taking too long in answering any single question – Remember to time your answers properly

EXAMINATION SECTION

EVALUATING CONCLUSIONS IN LIGHT OF KNOWN FACTS

An ability needed in many state jobs is the ability to decide if a conclusion is true, based on a set of facts. (These questions can also be called "Logic".) First read the facts (or premises) that are given, and then look at the conclusion. Assume the facts are true, and decide if the conclusion is:

   1. Necessarily true.
   2. Probably, but not necessarily true.
   3. Indeterminable, cannot be determined.
   4. Probably, but not necessarily false.
   5. Necessarily false.

These five answer choices (above) are the same for each inference question.

1. FACTS: If the Commission approves the new proposal, the agency will move to a new location immediately. If the agency moves, five new supervisors will be appointed immediately. The Commission approved the new proposal.

    CONCLUSION: No new supervisors were appointed.

      1. Necessarily true.
      2. Probably, but not necessarily true.
      3. Indeterminable, cannot be determined.
      4. Probably, but not necessarily false.
      5. Necessarily false.

2. FACTS: If the director retires, John Jackson, the associate director, will not be transferred to another agency. Jackson will be promoted to director if he is not transferred. The director retired.

    CONCLUSION: Jackson will be promoted to director.

      1. Necessarily true.
      2. Probably, but not necessarily true.
      3. Indeterminable, cannot be determined.
      4. Probably, but not necessarily false.
      5. Necessarily false.

3. FACTS: If the maximum allowable income for food stamp recipients is increased, the number of food stamp recipients will increase. If the number of food stamp recipients increases, more funds must be allocated to the food stamp program, which will require a tax increase. Taxes cannot be raised without the approval of Congress. Congress probably will not approve a tax increase.

   CONCLUSION: The maximum allowable income for food stamp recipients will increase.

   1. Necessarily true.
   2. Probably, but not necessarily true.
   3. Indeterminable, cannot be determined.
   4. Probably, but not necessarily false.
   5. Necessarily false.

4. FACTS: If prices are raised and sales remain constant, profits will increase. Prices were raised and sales levels will probably be maintained.

   CONCLUSION: Profits will increase.

   1. Necessarily true.
   2. Probably, but not necessarily true.
   3. Indeterminable, cannot be determined.
   4. Probably, but not necessarily false.
   5. Necessarily false.

5. FACTS: Some employees in the personnel department are technicians. Most of the technicians working in the personnel department are test development specialists. Lisa Jones works in the personnel department.

   CONCLUSION: Lisa Jones is a technician.

   1. Necessarily true.
   2. Probably, but not necessarily true.
   3. Indeterminable, cannot be determined.
   4. Probably, but not necessarily false.
   5. Necessarily false.

INFERENCE QUESTION ANSWERS AND EXPLANATIONS

1. The correct answer is number 5 (necessarily false). The new proposal was approved. According to the facts, approval means that the agency will move, and moving to a new location means that five new supervisors will be appointed.

2. The correct answer is number 1 (necessarily true). According to the facts, the director retired, which means that Jackson will not be transferred and, therefore, will be promoted to director.

3. The correct answer is number 4 (probably, but not necessarily false). Since Congress probably will not approve a tax increase, the maximum allowable income for food stamp recipients probably will not increase.

4. The correct answer is number 2 (probably, but not necessarily true). According to the facts, profits will increase if prices are raised and sales remain constant. It is known that prices were raised. Although sales level will probably be maintained, this is not certain.

5. The correct answer is number 3 (indeterminable, cannot be determined). The facts give no indication of the proportion of employees who are technicians. Therefore, no conclusion can be drawn with respect to the probability that any one employee is a technician.

LOGICAL REASONING
EVALUATING CONCLUSIONS IN LIGHT OF KNOWN FACTS

EXAMINATION SECTION
TEST 1

DIRECTIONS: For the following questions, select the letter before the statement below which BEST expresses the relationship between the facts and the conclusion. Mark your answer:
- A. The facts prove the conclusion; or
- B. The facts disprove the conclusion; or
- C. The facts neither prove nor disprove the conclusion.

PRINT THE LETTER OF THE CORRECT ANSWER IN THE SPACE AT THE RIGHT.

1. FACTS: Andy types half as fast as Bill. Bill types twice as slow as Charlie. Bill types 60 words a minute.

   CONCLUSION: Charlie types 30 words a minute.

   1.____

2. FACTS: If Albert gets traded to the Cubs, Chris will have to be traded to the Padres. Albert will avoid being traded only if he hits a home run in his turn at bat. If Chris goes to the Padres, Dave will be traded to the Dodgers. Albert strikes out in this crucial at-bat.

   CONCLUSION: Dave gets traded to the Dodgers.

   2.____

3. FACTS: All beads are forms of jewelry. All jewelry is expensive. Everyone loves expensive beads.

   CONCLUSION: All beads are expensive.

   3.____

4. FACTS: No shrimp are mussels. Mussels are bivalves. All mussels have shells.

   CONCLUSION: Therefore, no shrimp have shells.

   4.____

5. FACTS: On their latest diet, Abby, Bea, Celia, and Donna lost a combined total of 260 pounds. Abby lost twice as much as Celia. Celia lost half as much as the woman who lost the most. Donna lost 80 pounds.

   CONCLUSION: Abby lost 100 pounds; Bea, 30; Celia, 50; and Donna, 80.

   5.____

6. FACTS: Ann's office is two floors above Brenda's.
   Brenda's office is one floor below the only woman in the building whose birthday is today. Sally's office is on the third floor. Ann's office is on the fourth floor.

   CONCLUSION: Today is Ann's birthday.

   6.____

7. FACTS: Douglas Ave. is perpendicular to Bates St. Bates St. is parallel to Adams Ave. Douglas Ave. is parallel to Charles St. Evans Ave. is parallel to the streets that are perpendicular to Bates St.

   CONCLUSION: Evans Ave. is perpendicular to Douglas Ave.

   7.____

5

8. FACTS: There's one out, and Bill is the runner on third base. If Arnie hits the ball hard, Bill will run, but so slowly that he will be out at home plate. The team captain, on second base, will not run unless Arnie hits the ball hard. The captain runs.

   CONCLUSION: Bill is safe.

9. FACTS: Some members of this genus are members of that species. All members of that species are butterflies. Some butterflies are different from others.

   CONCLUSION: Some members of this genus are butterflies.

10. FACTS: Some woodwinds are clarinets. Flutes are not clarinets. All clarinets are beautiful things.

    CONCLUSION: Therefore, all beautiful things are woodwinds.

11. FACTS: Using a grid exactly like the one below, Joe Genius filled in the numbers 1 through 9 in the boxes. Each horizontal, vertical, and diagonal row added up to 15. A different number went in each box.

    CONCLUSION: The number Joe put in the middle box was 6.

12. FACTS: Max, Nick, Pete, and Ollie all bought different colored suits: grey, green, blue, and brown, but not necessarily respectively. Max paid less for his green suit than Nick paid for his suit. Ollie paid twice what Pete paid. Pete paid the same as the man who bought the grey suit. Ollie bought the brown suit.

    CONCLUSION: Ollie paid the most.

13. FACTS: Four people (Alice, Bob, Carol, and Dave) are sitting at a square table, discussing their favorite sports. Bob sits directly across from the jogger. Carol sits to the right of the basketball player. Alice sits across from Dave. The golfer sits to the left of the tennis player. A man sits on Dave's right.

    CONCLUSION: Dave plays golf.

14. FACTS: An employer decided to offer a job to everyone who scored higher than 50 on an exam. Alice scored 20. Betty scored lower than Carol, but more than twice as high as Alice.

    CONCLUSION: Of the three women, only Carol was offered the job.

15. FACTS: If Camille's squirrel has rabies and the squirrel bites Casey's cat, the squirrel will have to be caught and the cat will get rabies. If the cat has had rabies shots within the last two years, the cat will not get rabies. Casey's cat did not get rabies.

    CONCLUSION: Casey's cat has had rabies shots within the last two years.

    15.____

16. FACTS: Sally will file a grievance only if Bill fires her. If Laura tells Frank the whole story, Frank will tell it to Bill. If Bill hears the whole story, he will not fire Sally. Laura tells Fred the whole story.

    CONCLUSION: Sally files a grievance.

    16.____

17. FACTS: If Alice leaves work early, Barb has to work late, and Barb wants to go to the game tonight. The singing of the National Anthem always precedes the game. Carl calls Alice and asks her out to dinner. Due to a thunderstorm, the singing of the National Anthem gets delayed. If Alice goes out to dinner with Carl, she will have to leave work early so she can go home and turn off her crockpot. Alice accepts Carl's invitation.

    CONCLUSION: Barb misses the first inning of the game.

    17.____

18. FACTS: Earl thinks of any whole number from 1 through 10. Because she is using the most efficient system, Eva absolutely guarantees Earl that she can correctly guess the number he's thinking of in five questions or less. Eva asks Earl a series of *yes/no* questions and guesses the number in five questions or less every time. Earl and Eva agree to play the game again in the exact same way, except that he will think of a whole number from 1 through 6.

    CONCLUSION: Using the same system, four is the absolute highest number of *yes/no* questions that Eva will need to ask in order to guess the number that Earl is thinking of this time.

    18.____

19. FACTS: Lois will cook dinner today only if Ted, Robbie, and Jennifer are all home by 6 P.M. Robbie will come home by 6 P.M. only if band practice ends early. If Ted plays Softball after work, he will take Jennifer with him, and they will not be home by 6 P.M. Band practice ends early today.

    CONCLUSION: Lois cooks dinner today.

    19.____

20. FACTS: Three card players each start with $10. Each round they play has two losers and one winner. The losers in each round have to give the winner $2 apiece. Chuck wins the first and third rounds; Bruce wins the second. At the end of the third round, Artie proposes that they change the rules so that the losers each have to give the winner half their accumulated money. They agree, play one more round, and Artie wins it.

    CONCLUSION: At the end of the fourth round, Chuck has less money than Artie.

    20.____

21. FACTS: No part-time workers at this plant get paid vacations. All cleaners at this plant are part-time workers. Joe gets a paid vacation.

    CONCLUSION: All cleaners at this plant get paid vacations.

    21.____

22. FACTS: If Myles breaks the lamp, Lucy will scream. If Tom finds Rachel spraying Windex into the cat's dish, he'll scream. If Geoffrey doesn't hear from the French soon, he'll scream. Tom screams.

    22.____

CONCLUSION: Myles broke the lamp.

23. FACTS: If Tina goes to the store, Ike will go with her. If Ike goes to the store, he will buy doughnuts. If Dick cleans the house, Sally will go to the store. If Sally goes to the store, Tina will go with her. Dick cleans the house.

    CONCLUSION: Ike buys doughnuts.

24. FACTS: If Joe passes the test, Jill won't apply for the job. If Jill applies for the job, she'll get it. If Jill doesn't apply for the job, Jeanne will be annoyed. Joe passes the test.

    CONCLUSION: Jeanne gets annoyed.

25. FACTS: Mary, Debbie, May, and Joan are the only people waiting for the photocopier to be fixed. When it's fixed, Debbie has to use it first because she's doing work for the boss. Joan has to use it right after the person who's been waiting the longest. The person who has the most work to copy gets to use the machine second. May has been waiting the longest. The person who has been waiting longest is not the person who has the most work to copy.

    CONCLUSION: Joan gets to use the photocopier third.

KEY (CORRECT ANSWERS)

1.	B		11.	B
2.	A		12.	A
3.	A		13.	A
4.	C		14.	C
5.	C		15.	C
6.	B		16.	C
7.	B		17.	C
8.	B		18.	A
9.	A		19.	C
10.	C		20.	A

21. B
22. C
23. A
24. A
25. B

SOLUTIONS

1. **CORRECT ANSWER: B**
   This is an easy problem if you read it carefully. The third sentence says that Bill types 60 words a minute; the second sentence says that Bill types twice as slow as Charlie. If Bill types twice as slow as Charlie, then Charlie types twice as fast as Bill, or 2 x 60. This means that Charlie types 120 words a minute, not 30 words a minute. These two sentences alone are all you need to disprove the conclusion; the first sentence is just a decoy. If you had *fallen for it* and misread the paragraph, you would most likely have chosen A. You probably would have skimmed the second sentence and assumed that it said *twice as fast*, just because the first sentence said *half as fast*.

2. **CORRECT ANSWER: A**
   This question may look more difficult than it is because the facts are thrown together haphazardly. Many of these logic questions present the *facts* in a very strange fashion. No one would ever talk like this in real life - at least not if they wanted to be understood. The point, of course, is to see how well you can sift through these things, avoid the pitfalls, and find the *truth* of the matter. If you approach a question carefully and attack it systematically, you will usually find that it is not really all that difficult. In this case, by studying the facts, you can see that Albert gets traded. He needs a home run to avoid being traded (sentence 2), but he strikes out in his at-bat (sentence 4). You can assume that this is the at-bat that determines his future because of the way the fourth sentence is worded. It uses the words, *this crucial at-bat.* Knowing the sad truth that he's been traded, you can then trace the chain of events: Chris goes to the Padres (sentence 1), which means that Dave goes to the Dodgers (sentence 3). So the conclusion is, indeed, proved by the facts given to us.

3. **CORRECT ANSWER: A**
   This is a classic form of logic problem, and, like question 2, it doesn't correspond to reality. We all know perfectly well that some beads are cheap, but that has NO bearing on this problem. You often have to let go of your common sense and experience when doing problems like these. Just stick to the facts as they are stated in the problem. The first two sentences are given as facts, and they are enough to prove the conclusion that *all beads are expensive.* In any problem where you are told that a given fact is all-inclusive, such as that *all A are B,* you can just substitute A for B in any other factual sentence in the problem. What is true of B is true of A. Therefore, when you come across another all-inclusive *truth,* such as *all B are C,* you know that *all A are C* must be true too.
   Here are two examples. Although only one corresponds to reality as we know it, they both follow the logic formula we've outlined above, and so both are *true* according to logic.

         All dogs (A) are mammals (B).
         All mammals (B) have backbones (C).
         All dogs (A) have backbones (C).

         All apples (A) are bananas (B).
         All bananas (B) have yellow skins (C).
         All apples (A) have yellow skins (C).

Note that this does not work in reverse. All bananas aren't necessarily apples, all things with yellow skins aren't necessarily bananas or apples, and all mammals aren't necessarily dogs. Don't worry if this is confusing to you. The key here is to know the formula and not think about it too much in terms of reality.

In this problem, the *A* is the beads, the *B* is the jewelry, and the *C* is expensive.

4. CORRECT ANSWER: C
This looks a lot like the previous question, but, in fact, the sentences show no relationship between shrimp and shells. You can eliminate the second sentence because it has nothing at all to do with the conclusion. Of the two remaining sentences, one says that mussels have shells, the other says that no shrimp are mussels. This doesn't tell us that <u>no shrimp have shells</u> because it is not really telling us anything about how these two animals compare with each other on this issue. It's as if we said, *all boys like sports* and *no boys are girls*. These statements don't tell us whether girls like sports. They tell us that boys and girls are different, but we don't know how different they are. Are they completely different, or do they have things in common? Is liking sports one of the ways they differ or one of the ways they are alike?

For this reason, there is also nothing in the question to show that shrimp <u>do have shells.</u> Here we have another case where common sense can get you into trouble. You may want to choose answer B, simply because you know that the conclusion is false. But you are <u>not</u> being asked whether the conclusion is true or false; you are being asked whether it is <u>proved</u> true or false <u>by the facts as given</u>. If sentence 3 had said, *only mussels have shells,* then the facts would prove the conclusion, even if that doesn't correspond to reality. But as it is, the facts neither prove nor disprove the conclusion.

5. CORRECT ANSWER: C
This is a tricky one. You may have added all the pounds in the conclusion, and been relieved to find that they totaled the 260 pounds mentioned in the first sentence. You would have been tricked into picking A because the numbers checked out. But it doesn't matter that the numbers match because the problem here is to decide whether the facts <u>prove</u> that those are the exact number of pounds <u>each</u> woman lost. And the facts show that, without knowing Bea's weight loss, we're sure of only one figure - Donna's 80-pound weight loss. This is shown below:

NAME	AMOUNT LOST
Abby	2 x Celia
Bea	?
Celia	1/2 of Abby
Donna	80

You may have tried to work the problem by assuming that Donna's 80 pounds was the highest amount lost because that clue is contained in the problem. If Donna's 80 pounds were the greatest weight loss, Celia would have lost 40 pounds because sentence 3 says that Celia lost half of the greatest amount lost. But this creates a problem because it would mean that Abby also lost 80. Sentence 2 says Abby lost twice what Celia lost. And Abby COULDN'T have lost 80 pounds because that would mean that two women (Abby and Donna) lost the most. This is impossible because sentence 3 says Celia lost half as

10

much as the woman (not women) who lost the most. So the greatest amount lost must have been more than 80 pounds, and Abby must have been the one who lost it. All we know, then, is the following: Donna lost 80 pounds, the greatest amount lost was more than 80 pounds, Celia's amount was half the greatest amount, and Abby lost more than 80 pounds. As long as all these conditions are met, Bea's loss might be any amount that makes up the difference between 260 and the others' total weight loss. For example, the losses could have been:

Abby	84		Abby	90		Abby	94
Bea	54	OR	Bea	45	OR	Bea	39
Celia	42		Celia	45		Celia	47
Donna	80		Donna	80		Donna	80
	260			260			260

Or many other possible combinations. The facts simply don't give us enough information to either prove or disprove that the amounts given in the conclusion are the actual amounts each woman lost. That's why the correct answer is C.

6. CORRECT ANSWER: B
To see why B is the correct answer, it is helpful to draw a diagram of the floors. We know that Ann is on Four (sentence 4) and that Sally is on Three (sentence 3). If Ann is two floors above Brenda (sentence 1), Brenda must be on Two. Now we can draw:

Ann - - - - - - - - - - - - - - (4)
Sally - - - - - - - - - - - - - (3)
Brenda - - - - - - - - - - - - (2)

So, if Brenda is one floor below the birthday-girl (sentence 2), today must be Sally's birthday, not Ann's.

7. CORRECT ANSWER: B
Here, you need to know what perpendicular and parallel mean. If you do, a simple diagram should show you that the facts disprove the conclusion. Perpendicular streets are those at right angles to one another, like the two lines in a plus sign (+). Parallel streets are those that run in the same direction, never touching - like the two l's in the word all. The first three facts tell us that the streets look like this:

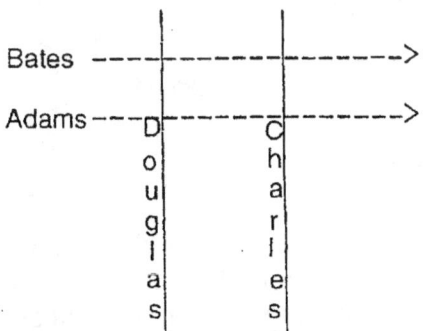

If Evans is parallel to the streets that are perpendicular to Bates (sentence 4), then Evans itself must be perpendicular to Bates. The completed diagram now looks like this:

8 (#1)

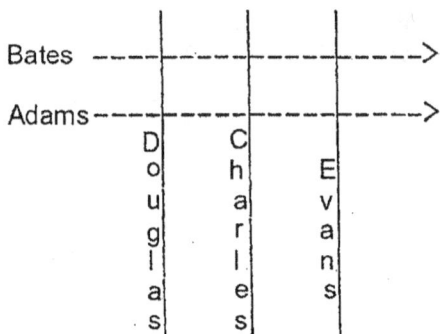

This diagram graphically shows that Evans is NOT perpendicular to Douglas, but parallel to it. The facts, then, disprove the conclusion.

8. **CORRECT ANSWER: B**
   If you start from the last fact given in this problem and work backwards, you will be able to find the cause of each event. This will enable you to either prove or disprove the conclusion. In this case, since the last fact says that the captain ran, that must have been because Arnie hit the ball hard (sentence 3). Even though Arnie hit the ball hard, Bill is out because Bill is so slow that he will be out at home plate (sentence 2). This disproves the conclusion, which says he is safe.

9. **CORRECT ANSWER: A**
   This is an easy problem if you translate the facts into a picture. First of all, ignore sentence 3, which has nothing to do with the problem. Now, draw a circle to represent all the members of this genus (sentence 1). Next, draw a smaller circle to represent the members of that species (sentence 1). You may know that a species is a subgroup of a genus, just as *semi-precious* is a subgroup of gems, or hardwoods is a subgroup of trees. For this reason, the *species* circle should be contained entirely within the *genus* circle. The problem doesn't tell you this about genus and species, but you don't need to know it to answer the question correctly. You could simply place the smaller circle partially in and partially out of the larger circle. No matter which way you portray the relationship, some members of the genus will belong to that species. You can see this in the diagrams below. Since all members of that species are butterflies (sentence 2), the *species* circle also represents butterflies.

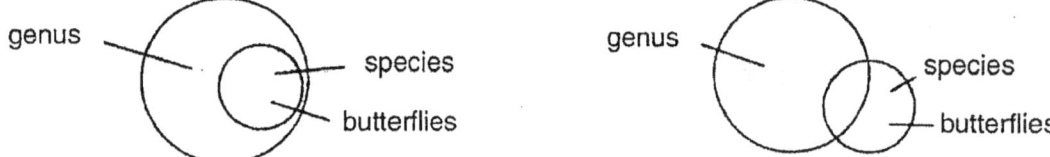

Not <u>all</u> members of this genus are butterflies; this is demonstrated by the fact that there is plenty of room inside the *genus* circle for other, non-butterfly critters. But the picture clearly shows that <u>some</u> members of the genus are butterflies, as the conclusion states.

10. **CORRECT ANSWER: C**
The facts prove only that some woodwinds (those that are clarinets) are beautiful things; they do not prove that all beautiful things are woodwinds. If you draw circles to represent *beautiful things* and *clarinets,* the latter would have to be a smaller circle inside the former, since all clarinets are beautiful things (sentence 3).

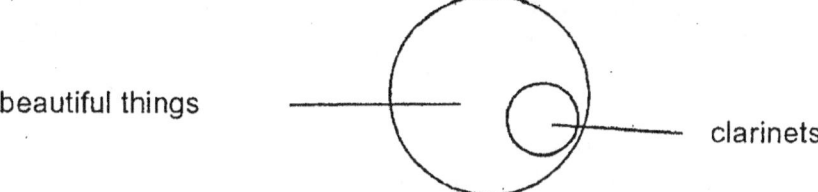

But where does the *woodwind* circle go? All the facts tell us is that some of its members are clarinets. We don't know whether it's bigger, smaller, or the same size as the circle of *beautiful things*. It could look like the following:

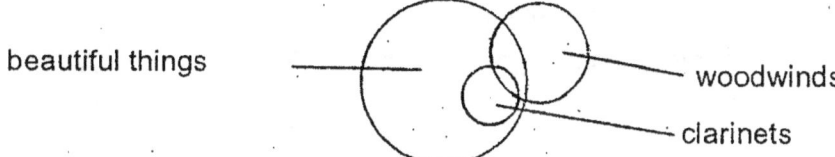

That way, there could be plenty of beautiful things that are not woodwinds, some beautiful things that are woodwinds and clarinets, and some woodwinds that are beautiful things but not clarinets. And the conclusion would be false.
OR, the *woodwinds* circle could be identical to the *beautiful things* circle:

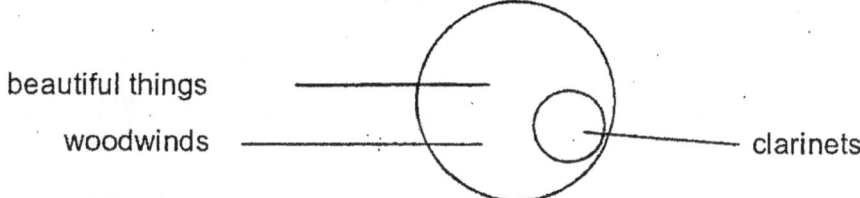

making the conclusion true.
You may have circled answer B, simply because the conclusion is obviously a false statement. But remember, the question is not whether the conclusion is true or false; it's whether it is proved or disproved by the facts given. In this case, it is neither proved nor disproved by the facts. Sentence 2, incidentally, is irrelevant, since the rest of the problem has nothing to do with flutes.

11. CORRECT ANSWER: B
You could use a trial-and-error approach to this problem, but it would be very time-consuming. As you worked with this problem, you may have realized that, since the number in the middle box gets added to every other number, you can solve the problem more easily by putting 6 into the diagram and adding the larger numbers to it to see if it's workable. After placing 6 in the center, you can see there is nowhere to put 9. The horizontal, vertical, and diagonal rows must add up to 15, but wherever you try to put 9, you will have a row that adds up to more than 15. Since 9 + 6 = 15 and 0 is not one of the options, there is no number that can be put in the third box in the row.

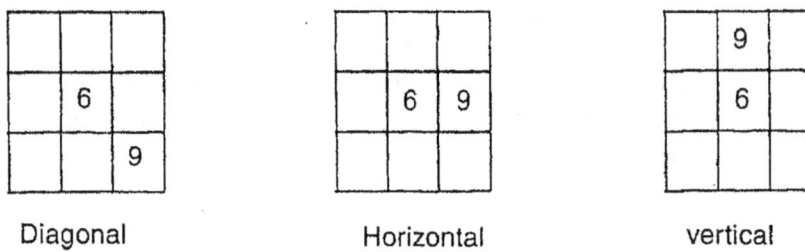

Diagonal   Horizontal   vertical

So, 6 cannot be the number in the middle box; it's too big. The facts disprove the conclusion.

12. CORRECT ANSWER: A
The first sentence in this problem says that these men bought various colored suits, but not necessarily <u>respectively</u>. This means that the first man (Max) didn't necessarily buy the first color suit (grey), the second man (Nick) didn't necessarily buy the second color suit (green), and so on. <u>Respectively</u> means *in the same order*.
At first glance, this problem looks impossible, but it can be simplified by drawing a chart to show what we *know* about each person:

NAME	PAID	FOR THIS COLOR SUIT
Max	less than Nick	green
Nick	same as Pete	grey (not green, brown or blue)
Pete	same as Nick	blue (not grey, green or brown)
Ollie	2x Nick; 2x Pete	brown

Sentence 2 says Max's suit is green, and sentence 5 says Ollie's is brown, but how do we know Pete's is blue? Well, sentence 4 indicates that someone other than Pete bought the grey one. That means Nick got the grey one. Since the grey, green, and brown suits are all accounted for, the blue one must be Pete's.

Now, all we need to know is who paid the most! Ollie paid twice what Pete paid (sentence 3). This means that he also paid twice what Nick paid because Pete paid the same as the man who bought the grey suit (sentence 4) - and Nick bought the grey suit. So the highest-payer can't be Nick or Pete; it must either be Ollie or Max. But sentence 2 says Max paid <u>less</u> than Nick. So the highest-payer must be Ollie, as proved by the facts given.

13. **CORRECT ANSWER: A**

The man sitting on Dave's right (sentence 6) has to be Bob because he's the only other man in the group. Alice sits across from Dave (sentence 4). This means that Carol must be sitting across from Bob. From this information, you can draw a diagram of the table and the people seated at it:

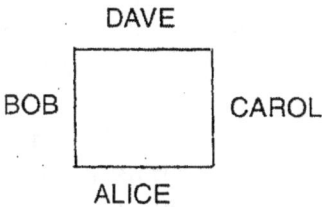

Now all you need to know is whether Dave plays golf. It may help keep everything straight if you put the name of the sport next to the name of the proper person as you figure out each one. Here, we have abbreviated each sport using a lower-case initial (*j* for jogging, *g* for golf, and so on). Since Carol sits to the right of the basketball player (sentence 3), Alice must play basketball. (Remember, it's not Carol's right; it's the basketball player's right. This confuses some people.) Since Bob sits across from the jogger (sentence 2), Carol must jog. After adding this information, your diagram would look like this:

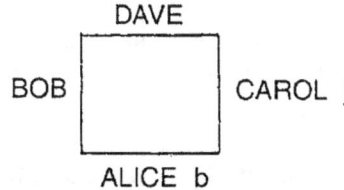

At this point, all you need to know is: Does Bob golf and Dave play tennis, or is it the other way around? A quick trial-and-error produces the answer. Sentence 5 says the golfer sits to the left of the tennis player. If Dave played tennis, would this be true? No. So, it must be Bob who's the tennis player, and Dave who's the golfer. The conclusion is thus proved by the facts. If you have spatial problems, you might want to twist the diagram around to see this more clearly.

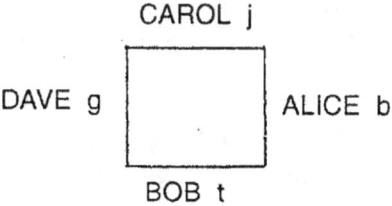

14. **CORRECT ANSWER: C**

To visualize this problem it is helpful to draw a small chart, showing what we know about each woman's score.

NAME	SCORE
Carol	higher than Betty

Betty	higher than 40 (according to sentence 3 she scored more than twice as high as Alice
Alice	20

From this chart, we can see that Carol's score could have been <u>any</u> number higher than 41. It could have been 50, or 65, or 92–in which case she would have scored high enough to be hired. But it also could have been 42, or 43, or 47–in which case she would not have scored high enough. So, we can't prove that Carol was offered the job, but we can't prove that she wasn't either. In addition, we can't prove that Carol was the only one who was offered the job. We know Alice didn't get an offer (with a score of 20), but we don't know about Betty. She could have gotten anything above 40. So, the facts here neither prove nor disprove the conclusion.

15. CORRECT ANSWER: C
    This is a sneaky little question. If you read it quickly, you might have thought it was easy. The cat didn't get rabies (sentence 3), so the cat had had its rabies shots within the last two years (sentence 2). But perhaps the cat didn't get rabies because the squirrel never bit it, or perhaps the squirrel never had rabies to begin with. The first sentence says, <u>If Camille's squirrel has rabies"</u> and <u>(if)</u> the squirrel bites Casey's cat...the cat will get rabies. (The second if is implied by the structure of the sentence.) Nothing in this paragraph ever tells us that the squirrel had rabies or that the squirrel bit the cat. As we said - sneaky. Since you don't know why the cat didn't get rabies, you can't prove that it was spared because it had had its shots, and you can't disprove it either. Therefore, C is the only possible answer.

16. CORRECT ANSWER: C
    This is another sneaky question. (The exams haven't used this kind of trick lately, but we wanted to give you practice – just in case.) If you didn't read the problem carefully, you might have chosen B. You would have thought that Laura told Frank (sentence 4), who told Bill (sentence 2), who chose not to fire Sally (sentence 3). Since Sally didn't get fired, she didn't file a grievance (sentence 1). The only problem is that Laura told <u>Fred</u>, not Frank, and we have no way of knowing how Fred fits into this crew. He could have told Frank, thereby setting in motion the cycle above and preventing Sally from getting fired. In that case, the conclusion would be false. Or he could have not told anyone, Sally would have gotten fired, she would have filed a grievance, and the conclusion would have been true. You just don't know, so C is the only option.

17. CORRECT ANSWER: C
    Obviously, if the *pre-game* song gets delayed, the game will also be delayed, but we don't know for how long. We also don't know how late Barb had to work. (We know that she <u>did</u> have to work late, because of sentences 1, 5, and 6.) For all we know, the game may have been delayed for an hour due to the storm, and Barb may have had to work only a half hour later than usual–thereby not missing any of the game at all. In questions of this type, it is always good to work backwards from the conclusion and try to see if there is a cause of that conclusion contained in the facts. In this case, although we can find a cause for Barb's having to work late (Alice's acceptance of Carl's invitation), we can find nothing that would <u>necessarily</u> cause Barb to miss the first inning of the game.

18. CORRECT ANSWER: A
    The conclusion seems likely because it only takes Eva five tries to guess a number from 1 through 10. The most efficient way to guess is to eliminate half of all possible numbers with each guess. When the number is from 1 through 10, the first question should be, *Is the number you're thinking of 6 or more?* The answer to that question, whether it's yes or no, will eliminate five numbers - half of all the numbers Earl could possibly be thinking of. Let's say Earl said yes. The second question would be, *Is it 8 or more?* That answer will eliminate two or three of the five remaining possible numbers. No matter what range of numbers Earl wants to use, whether it be 1 through 50, 1 through 100, or whatever, Eva could use this method until she narrows the answers down to one possible number. (We can assume that she uses this method because sentence 2 says she is using the most efficient method.)

    For the range 1 through 6, then, you can see that four is the highest number of guesses she will need using this system. The most she can be sure of eliminating with one guess is 3 numbers. *(Is the number you're thinking of 4 or more?)* At that point, she may need as many as three more guesses to eliminate the two remaining wrong numbers one by one and then to *guess* the right number. Since this is four guesses, the facts prove the conclusion.

19. CORRECT ANSWER: C
    Here is a case in which it is clear that certain facts are missing. You know from sentences 4 and 2 that Robbie is home in time for Lois to make dinner, but what about Ted and Jennifer? Nowhere in the facts does it say whether or not Ted played softball after work. Since sentence 1 says Lois will cook only if all three are home by 6 P.M., we simply don't have enough information to either prove or disprove the conclusion.

20. CORRECT ANSWER: A
    Unless you are excellent in math, just about the only way to figure this one out is to set up a grid showing the amount of money each player has after each round. After setting up such a grid, the answer can be found quite easily.

	ARTIE $10	BRUCE $10	CHUCK $10
AFTER ROUND #1	$8	$8	$14
#2	$6	$12	$12
#3	$4	$10	$16
#4	$17	$5	$8

    Chuck won the first round (sentence 4). Since everyone started with $10 (sentence 1), you can see that after Round #1, each loser would be out $2 (sentences 2 and 3), bringing their totals down to $8 each. Chuck, on the other hand, would be up to $14, having collected $2 from each of the two losers. The second line of the grid shows the situation after Round #2, which was won by Bruce (sentence 4). The third line shows the situation after Round #3, when Chuck is way ahead (sentence 4). Likewise, the fourth line shows the situation after Round #4, when the rules had been changed and Artie won (sentences 5 and 6). Since each of the other two had to give him half their money (sentence 5), he collected $5 from Bruce and $8 from Chuck. His total of $17 was $9 more than

Chuck had at that point. So, the conclusion that Artie ended up with more money than Chuck is proven by the facts given.

21. CORRECT ANSWER: B
The facts prove just the opposite of the conclusion. If all cleaners work part-time (sentence 2), and no part-timers get paid vacations (sentence 1), then no cleaners can get paid vacations. Where *facts* are given in the form, *No A are B, and all C are A,* you can simply substitute C for A, and that will prove that no C are B. (This is much like question 3, except the first fact is all-exclusive rather than all-inclusive. It excludes rather than includes all of something. See the explanation to question 3, if this is not clear.) In this case, *A* is the part-timers, *B* represents recipients of paid vacations, and *C* is cleaners. The facts disprove the conclusion. Since we don't know what Joe's occupation is, sentence 3 is irrelevant to this problem.

22. CORRECT ANSWER: C
In this case, no amount of *following the trail* of facts will lead you to the conclusion given because there is no trail. No fact implies, or leads to, any other; they are simply a collection of statements with no relationship to one another. The facts neither prove nor disprove the conclusion.

23. CORRECT ANSWER: A
Unlike question 22, this question lends itself to *following the trail* of facts. As we've noticed earlier, a good place to begin the trail is with the last fact. It follows from sentence 5 (Dick cleans the house) that Sally goes to the store (sentence 3), which means that Tina also goes to the store (sentence 4). This, in turn, means that Ike goes (sentence 1), and buys the doughnuts (sentence 2). The facts here prove the conclusion.

24. CORRECT ANSWER: A
To decide whether the facts prove the conclusion, you must understand what each fact means. The fact that Joe passed the test (sentence 4) means that Jill didn't apply for the job (sentence 1). Knowing this, all you have to do is reread sentence 3 to see that Jeanne does, indeed, get annoyed. Sentence 2 is not needed to solve this problem, although it may explain why Jeanne got annoyed.

25. CORRECT ANSWER: B
It is helpful to make a list of who's using the machine when, and to fill in the facts you're given. Then you can gradually deduce more information, until you can see whether the conclusion is proved, disproved, or neither. Sentence 2 says Debbie goes first, so your list, at the start, would look something like this:

>First - Debbie
>Second - ?
>Third - ?
>Last - ?

It is clear from sentences 3 and 5 that Joan immediately follows May. This also means that Joan cannot be second, May cannot be last, and Mary cannot be third. You may then wish to enter the possibilities to your list:

>First - Debbie
>Second - May or Mary

15 (#1)

> Third - May or Joan
> Last - Joan or Mary

Now, all we need to know is: Does May go second? If so, the conclusion is proved by the facts; if not, it's disproved. We know from sentence 4 that the person with the most work goes second. That person can't be May, however, because May has been waiting longest (sentence 5), and the longest-waiter is not the person with the most work (sentence 6). So, Debbie is first, Mary is second, May is third, Joan is fourth, and the conclusion is disproved.

> First - Debbie
> Second - Mary
> Third - May
> Last - Joan

EVALUATING CONCLUSIONS IN LIGHT OF KNOWN FACTS
EXAMINATION SECTION
TEST 1

DIRECTIONS: Each question or incomplete statement is followed by several suggested answers or completions. Select the one that BEST answers the question or completes the statement. *PRINT THE LETTER OF THE CORRECT ANSWER IN THE SPACE AT THE RIGHT.*

Questions 1-9.

DIRECTIONS: In Questions 1 through 9, you will read a set of facts and a conclusion drawn from them. The conclusion may be valid or invalid, based on the facts—it's your task to determine the validity of the conclusion.

For each question, select the letter before the statement that BEST expresses the relationship between the given facts and the conclusion that has been drawn from them. Your choices are:
   A. The facts prove the conclusion;
   B. The facts disprove the conclusion; or
   C. The facts neither prove nor disprove the conclusion.

1. FACTS: If the supervisor retires, James, the assistant supervisor, will not be transferred to another department. James will be promoted to supervisor if he is not transferred. The supervisor retired.

   CONCLUSION: James will be promoted to supervisor.
   A. The facts prove the conclusion.
   B. The facts disprove the conclusion.
   C. The facts neither prove nor disprove the conclusion.

2. FACTS: In the town of Luray, every player on the softball team works at Luray National Bank. In addition, every player on the Luray softball team wear glasses.

   CONCLUSIONS: At least some of the people who work at Luray National Bank wear glasses.
   A. The facts prove the conclusion.
   B. The facts disprove the conclusion.
   C. The facts neither prove nor disprove the conclusion.

3. FACTS: The only time Henry and June go out to dinner is on an evening when they have childbirth classes. Their childbirth classes meet on Tuesdays and Thursdays.

2 (#1)

CONCLUSION: Henry and June never go out to dinner on Friday or Saturday.
   A. The facts prove the conclusion.
   B. The facts disprove the conclusion.
   C. The facts neither prove nor disprove the conclusion.

4. FACTS: Every player on the field hockey team has at least one bruise. Everyone on the field hockey team also has scarred knees.

   CONCLUSION: Most people with both bruises and scarred knees are field hockey players.
   A. The facts prove the conclusion.
   B. The facts disprove the conclusion.
   C. The facts neither prove nor disprove the conclusion.

4.____

5. FACTS: In the chess tournament, Lance will win his match against Jane if Jane wins her match against Mathias. If Lance wins his match against Jane, Christine will not win her match against Jane.

   CONCLUSION: Christine will not win her match against Jane if Jane wins her match against Mathias.
   A. The facts prove the conclusion.
   B. The facts disprove the conclusion.
   C. The facts neither prove nor disprove the conclusion.

5.____

6. FACTS: No green lights on the machine are indicators for the belt drive status. Not all of the lights on the machine's upper panel are green. Some lights on the machine's lower panel are green.

   CONCLUSION: The green lights on the machine's lower panel may be indicators for the belt drive status.
   A. The facts prove the conclusion.
   B. The facts disprove the conclusion.
   C. The facts neither prove nor disprove the conclusion.

6.____

7. FACTS: At a small, one-room country school, there are eight students: Amy, Ben, Carla, Dan, Elliot, Francine, Greg, and Hannah. Each student is in either the 6th, 7th, or 8th grade. Either two or three students are in each grade. Amy, Dan, and Francine are all in different grades. Ben and Elliot are both in the 7th grade. Hannah and Carl are in the same grade.

   CONCLUSION: Exactly three students are in the 7th grade.
   A. The facts prove the conclusion.
   B. The facts disprove the conclusion.
   C. The facts neither prove nor disprove the conclusion.

7.____

8. FACTS: Two married couples are having lunch together. Two of the four people are German and two are Russian, but in each couple the nationality of the spouse is not necessarily the same as the other's. One person in the group is a teacher, the other a lawyer, one an engineer, and the other a writer. The teacher is a Russian man. The writer is Russian, and her husband is an engineer. One of the people, Mr. Stern, is German.

   CONCLUSION: Mr. Stern's wife is a writer.
   A. The facts prove the conclusion.
   B. The facts disprove the conclusion.
   C. The facts neither prove nor disprove the conclusion.

   8.____

9. FACTS: The flume ride at the county fair is open only to children who are at least 36 inches tall. Lisa is 30 inches tall. John is shorter than Henry, but more than 10 inches taller than Lisa.

   CONCLUSION: Lisa is the only one who can't ride the flume ride.
   A. The facts prove the conclusion.
   B. The facts disprove the conclusion.
   C. The facts neither prove nor disprove the conclusion.

   9.____

Questions 10-17.

DIRECTIONS: Questions 10 through 17 are based on the following reading passage. It is not your knowledge of the particular topic that is being tested, but your ability to reason based on what you have read. The passage is likely to detail several proposed courses of action and factors affecting these proposals. The reading passage is followed by a conclusion or outcome based on the facts in the passage, or a description of a decision taken regarding the situation. The conclusion is followed by a number of statements that have a possible connection to the conclusion. For each statement, you are to determine whether:
   A. The statement proves the conclusion.
   B. The statement supports the conclusion but does not prove it.
   C. The statement disproves the conclusion.
   D. The statement weakens the conclusion but does not disprove it.
   E. The statement has no relevance to the conclusion.

Remember that the conclusion after the passage is to be accepted as the outcome of what actually happened, and that you are being asked to evaluate the impact each statement would have had on the conclusion.

PASSAGE:

The Grand Army of Foreign Wars, a national veteran's organization, is struggling to maintain its National Home, where the widowed spouses and orphans of deceased members are housed together in a small village-like community. The Home is open to spouses and children who are bereaved for any reason, regardless of whether the member's death was related to military service, but a new global conflict has led to a dramatic surge in the number of members' deaths: many veterans who re-enlisted for the conflict have been killed in action.

The Grand Army of Foreign Wars is considering several options for handling the increased number of applications for housing at the National Home, which has been traditionally supported by membership due. At its national convention, it will choose only one of the following:

The first idea is a one-time $50 tax on all members, above and beyond the dues they pay already. Since the organization has more than a million member, this tax should be sufficient for the construction and maintenance of new housing for applicants on the existing grounds of the National Home. The idea is opposed, however, by some older members who live on fixed incomes. These members object in principle to the taxation of Grand Army members. The Grand Army has never imposed a tax on its members.

The second idea is to launch a national fundraising drive the public relations campaign that will attract donations for the National Home. Several national celebrities are members of the organization, and other celebrities could be attracted to the cause. Many Grand Army members are wary of this approach, however: in the past, the net receipts of some fundraising efforts have been relatively insignificant, given the costs of staging them.

A third approach, suggested by many of the younger members, is to have new applicants share some of the costs of construction and maintenance. The spouses and children would pay an up-front "enrollment" fee, based on a sliding scale proportionate to their income and assets, and then a monthly fee adjusted similarly to contribute to maintenance costs. Many older members are strongly opposed to this idea, as it is in direct contradiction to the principles on which the organization was founded more than a century ago.

The fourth option is simply to maintain the status quo, focus the organization's efforts on supporting the families who already live at the National Home, and wait to accept new applicants based on attrition.

CONCLUSION: At its annual national convention, the Grand Army of Foreign Wars votes to impose a one-time tax of $10 on each member for the purpose of expanding and supporting the National Home to welcome a larger number of applicants. The tax is considered to be the solution most likely to produce the funds needed to accommodate the growing number of applicants.

10. Actuarial studies have shown that because the Grand Army's membership consists mostly of older veterans from earlier wars, the organization's membership will suffer a precipitous decline in numbers in about five years.
    A. The statement proves the conclusion.
    B. The statement supports the conclusion but does not prove it.
    C. The statement disproves the conclusion.
    D. The statement weakens the conclusion but does not disprove it.
    E. The statement has no relevance to the conclusion.

11. After passage of the funding measure, a splinter group of older members appeals for the "sliding scale" provision to be applied to the tax, so that some members may be allowed to contribute less based on their income.
    A. The statement proves the conclusion.
    B. The statement supports the conclusion but does not prove it.
    C. The statement disproves the conclusion.
    D. The statement weakens the conclusion but does not disprove it.
    E. The statement has no relevance to the conclusion.

12. The original charter of the Grand Army of Foreign Wars specifically states that the organization will not levy taxes or duties on its members beyond its modest annual dues. It takes a super-majority of attending delegates at the national convention to make alterations to the charter.
    A. The statement proves the conclusion.
    B. The statement supports the conclusion but does not prove it.
    C. The statement disproves the conclusion.
    D. The statement weakens the conclusion but does not disprove it.
    E. The statement has no relevance to the conclusion.

12.____

13. Six months before Grand Army of Foreign Wars' national convention, the Internal Revenue Service rules that because it is an organization that engages in political lobbying, the Grand Army must no longer enjoy its own federal tax-exempt status.
    A. The statement proves the conclusion.
    B. The statement supports the conclusion but does not prove it.
    C. The statement disproves the conclusion.
    D. The statement weakens the conclusion but does not disprove it.
    E. The statement has no relevance to the conclusion.

13.____

14. Two months before the national convention, Dirk Rockwell, arguably the country's most famous film actor, announces in a nationally televised interview that he has been saddened to learn of the plight of the National Home, and that he is going to make it his own personal crusade to see that it is able to house and support a greater number of widowed spouses and orphans in the future.
    A. The statement proves the conclusion.
    B. The statement supports the conclusion but does not prove it.
    C. The statement disproves the conclusion.
    D. The statement weakens the conclusion but does not disprove it.
    E. The statement has no relevance to the conclusion.

14.____

15. The Grand Army's final estimate is that the cost of expanding the National Home to accommodate the increased number of applicants will be about $61 million.
    A. The statement proves the conclusion.
    B. The statement supports the conclusion but does not prove it.
    C. The statement disproves the conclusion.
    D. The statement weakens the conclusion but does not disprove it.
    E. The statement has no relevance to the conclusion.

15.____

16. Just before the national convention, the Federal Department of Veterans Affairs announces steep cuts in the benefits package that is currently offered to the widowed spouses and orphans of veterans.
    A. The statement proves the conclusion.
    B. The statement supports the conclusion but does not prove it.
    C. The statement disproves the conclusion.
    D. The statement weakens the conclusion but does not disprove it.
    E. The statement has no relevance to the conclusion.

16.____

17. After the national convention, the Grand Army of Foreign Wars begins charging a modest "start-up" fee to all families who apply for residence at the national home.
    A. The statement proves the conclusion.
    B. The statement supports the conclusion but does not prove it.
    C. The statement disproves the conclusion.
    D. The statement weakens the conclusion but does not disprove it.
    E. The statement has no relevance to the conclusion.

17.____

Questions 18-25.

DIRECTIONS: Questions 18 through 25 each provide four factual statements and a conclusion based on these statements. After reading the entire question, you will decide whether:
   A. The conclusion is proved by statements I-IV;
   B. The conclusion is disproved by statements I-IV.
   C. The facts are not sufficient to prove or disprove the conclusion.

18. FACTUAL STATEMENTS:
    I. In the Field Day high jump competition, Martha jumped higher than Frank.
    II. Carl jumped higher than Ignacio.
    III. Ignacio jumped higher than Frank.
    IV. Dan jumped higher than Carl.

    CONCLUSION: Frank finished last in the high jump competition.
    A. The conclusion is proved by statements I-IV;
    B. The conclusion is disproved by statements I-IV.
    C. The facts are not sufficient to prove or disprove the conclusion.

18.____

19. FACTUAL STATEMENTS:
    I. The door to the hammer mill chamber is locked if light 6 is red.
    II. The door to the hammer mill chamber is locked only when the mill is operating.
    III. If the mill is not operating, light 6 is blue.
    IV. Light 6 is blue.

    CONCLUSION: The door to the hammer mill chamber is locked.
    A. The conclusion is proved by statements I-IV;
    B. The conclusion is disproved by statements I-IV.
    C. The facts are not sufficient to prove or disprove the conclusion.

19.____

20. FACTUAL STATEMENTS:
    I. Ziegfried, the lion tamer at the circus, has demanded ten additional minutes of performance time during each show.
    II. If Ziegfried is allowed his ten additional minutes per show, he will attempt to teach Kimba the tiger to shoot a basketball.
    III. If Kimba learns how to shoot a basketball, then Ziegfried was not given his ten additional minutes.
    IV. Ziegfried was given his ten additional minutes.

20.____

7 (#1)

CONCLUSION: Despite Ziegfried's efforts, Kimba did not learn how to shoot a basketball.
   A. The conclusion is proved by statements I-IV;
   B. The conclusion is disproved by statements I-IV.
   C. The facts are not sufficient to prove or disprove the conclusion.

21. FACTUAL STATEMENTS: 21.____
   I. If Stan goes to counseling, Sara won't divorce him.
   II. If Sara divorces Stan, she'll move back to Texas.
   III. If Sara doesn't divorce Stan, Irene will be disappointed.
   IV. Stan goes to counseling.

CONCLUSION: Irene will be disappointed.
   A. The conclusion is proved by statements I-IV;
   B. The conclusion is disproved by statements I-IV.
   C. The facts are not sufficient to prove or disprove the conclusion.

22. FACTUAL STATEMENTS: 22.____
   I. If Delia is promoted to district manager, Claudia will have to be promoted to team leader.
   II. Delia will be promoted to district manager unless she misses her fourth-quarter sales quota.
   III. If Claudia is promoted to team leader, Thomas will be promoted to assistant team leader.
   IV. Delia meets her fourth-quarter sales quota.

CONCLUSION: Thomas is promoted to assistant team leader.
   A. The conclusion is proved by statements I-IV;
   B. The conclusion is disproved by statements I-IV.
   C. The facts are not sufficient to prove or disprove the conclusion.

23. FACTUAL STATEMENTS: 23.____
   I. Clone D is identical to Clone B.
   II. Clone B is not identical to Clone A.
   III. Clone D is not identical to Clone C.
   IV. Clone E is not identical to the clones that are identical to Clone B.

CONCLUSION: Clone E is identical to Clone D.
   A. The conclusion is proved by statements I-IV;
   B. The conclusion is disproved by statements I-IV.
   C. The facts are not sufficient to prove or disprove the conclusion.

24. FACTUAL STATEMENTS: 24.____
   I. In the Stafford Tower, each floor is occupied by a single business.
   II. Big G Staffing is on a floor between CyberGraphics and MainEvent.
   III. Gasco is on the floor directly below CyberGraphics and three floors above Treehorn Audio.
   IV. MainEvent is five floors below EZ Tax and four floors below Treehorn Audio.

8 (#1)

CONCLUSION: EZ Tax is on a floor between Gasco and MainEvent.
  A. The conclusion is proved by statements I-IV;
  B. The conclusion is disproved by statements I-IV.
  C. The facts are not sufficient to prove or disprove the conclusion.

25. FACTUAL STATEMENTS:
  I. Only county roads lead to Nicodemus.
  II. All the roads from Hill City to Graham County are federal highways.
  III. Some of the roads from Plainville lead to Nicodemus.
  IV. Some of the roads running from Hill City lead to Strong City.

  CONCLUSION: Some of the roads from Plainville are county roads.
  A. The conclusion is proved by statements I-IV;
  B. The conclusion is disproved by statements I-IV.
  C. The facts are not sufficient to prove or disprove the conclusion.

25._____

KEY (CORRECT ANSWERS)

1.	A		11.	A
2.	A		12.	D
3.	A		13.	E
4.	C		14.	D
5.	A		15.	B
6.	B		16.	B
7.	A		17.	C
8.	A		18.	A
9.	A		19.	B
10.	E		20.	A

21.	A
22.	A
23.	B
24.	A
25.	A

SOLUTIONS TO PROBLEMS

1. **CORRECT ANSWER: A**
   Given Statement 3, we deduce that James will not be transferred to another department. By Statement 2, we can conclude that James will be promoted.

2. **CORRECT ANSWER: A**
   Since every player on the softball team wears glasses, these individuals compose some of the people who work at the bank. Although not every person who works at the bank plays softball, those bank employees who do play softball wear glasses.

3. **CORRECT ANSWER: A**
   If Henry and June go out to dinner, we conclude that it must be on Tuesday or Thursday, which are the only two days when they have childbirth classes. This implies that if it is not Tuesday or Thursday, then this couple does not go out to dinner.

4. **CORRECT ANSWER: C**
   We can only conclude that if a person plays on the field hockey team, then he or she has both bruises and scarred knees. But there are probably a great number of people who have both bruises and scarred knees but do not play on the field hockey team. The given conclusion can neither be proven or disproven.

5. **CORRECT ANSWER: A**
   From statement 1, if Jane beats Mathias, then Lance will beat Jane. Using statement 2, we can then conclude that Christine will not win her match against Jane.

6. **CORRECT ANSWER: B**
   Statement 1 tells us that no green light can be an indicator of the belt drive status. Thus, the given conclusion must be false.

7. **CORRECT ANSWER: A**
   We already know that Ben and Elliot are in the 7th grade. Even though Hannah and Carl are in the same grade, it cannot be the 7th grade because we would then have at least four students in this 7th grade. This would contradict the third statement, which states that either two or three students are in each grade. Since Amy, Dan, and Francine are in different grade, exactly one of them must be in the 7th grade. Thus, Ben, Elliot, and exactly one of Amy, Dan, and Francine are the three students in the 7th grade.

8. **CORRECT ANSWER: A**
   One man is a teacher, who is Russian. We know that the writer is female and is Russian. Since her husband is an engineer, he cannot be the Russian teacher. Thus, her husband is of German descent, namely Mr. Stern. This means that Mr. Stern's wife is the writer. Note that one couple consists of a male Russian teacher and a female German lawyer. The other couple consists of a male German engineer and a female Russian writer.

9. CORRECT ANSWER: A
Since John is more than 10 inches taller than Lisa, his height is at least 46 inches. Also, John is shorter than Henry, so Henry's height must be greater than 46 inches. Thus, Lisa is the only one whose height is less than 36 inches. Therefore, she is the only one who is not allowed on the flume ride.

18. CORRECT ANSWER: A
Dan jumped higher than Carl, who jumped higher than Ignacio, who jumped higher than Frank. Since Martha jumped higher than Frank, every person jumped higher than Frank. Thus, Frank finished last.

19. CORRECT ANSWER: B
If the light is red, then the door is locked. If the door is locked, then the mill is operating. Reversing the logical sequence of these statements, if the mill is not operating, then the door is not locked, which means that the light is blue. Thus, the given conclusion is disproved.

20. CORRECT ANSWER: A
Using the contrapositive of statement III, Ziegfried was given his ten additional minutes, then Kimba did not learn how to shoot a basketball. Since statement IV is factual, the conclusion is proved.

21. CORRECT ANSWER: A
From Statements IV and I, we conclude that Sara doesn't divorce Stan. Then statement III reveals that Irene will be disappointed. Thus, the conclusion is proved.

22. CORRECT ANSWER: A
Statement II can be rewritten as "Delia is promoted to district manager or she misses her sales quota." Furthermore, this statement is equivalent to "If Delia makes her sales quota, then she is promoted to district manager." From statement I, we conclude that Claudia is promoted to team leader. Finally, by statement III, Thomas is promoted to assistant team leader.

23. CORRECT ANSWER: B
By statement IV, Clone E is not identical to any clones identical to Clone B. Statement I tells us that Clones B and D are identical. Therefore, Clone E cannot be identical to Clone D. The conclusion is disproved.

24. CORRECT ANSWER: A
Based on all four statements, CyberGraphics is somewhere below MainEvent. Gasco is one floor below CyberGraphics. EZ Tax is two floors below Gasco. Treehorn Audio is one floor below EZ Tax. MainEvent is four floors below Treehorn Audio. Thus, EZ Tax is two floors below Gasco and five floors above MainEvent. The conclusion is proved.

25. CORRECT ANSWER: A
From statement III, we know that some of the roads from Plainville lead to Nicodemus. But statement I tells us that only county roads lead to Nicodemus. Therefore, some of the roads from Plainville must be county roads. The conclusion is proved.

TEST 2

DIRECTIONS: Each question or incomplete statement is followed by several suggested answers or completions. Select the one that BEST answers the question or completes the statement. *PRINT THE LETTER OF THE CORRECT ANSWER IN THE SPACE AT THE RIGHT.*

Questions 1-9.

DIRECTIONS: In Questions 1 through 9, you will read a set of facts and a conclusion drawn from them. The conclusion may be valid or invalid, based on the facts—it's your task to determine the validity of the conclusion.

For each question, select the letter before the statement that BEST expresses the relationship between the given facts and the conclusion that has been drawn from them. Your choices are:
   A. The facts prove the conclusion;
   B. The facts disprove the conclusion; or
   C. The facts neither prove nor disprove the conclusion.

1. FACTS: Some employees in the testing department are statisticians. Most of the statisticians who work in the testing department are projection specialists. Tom Wilks works in the testing department.

   CONCLUSION: Tom Wilks is a statistician.
   A. The facts prove the conclusion.
   B. The facts disprove the conclusion.
   C. The facts neither prove nor disprove the conclusion.

2. FACTS: Ten coins are split among Hank, Lawrence, and Gail. If Lawrence gives his coins to Hank, then Hank will have more coins than Gail. If Gail gives her coins to Lawrence, then Lawrence will have more coins than Hank.

   CONCLUSION: Hank has six coins.
   A. The facts prove the conclusion.
   B. The facts disprove the conclusion.
   C. The facts neither prove nor disprove the conclusion.

3. FACTS: Nobody loves everybody. Janet loves Ken. Ken loves everybody who loves Janet.

   CONCLUSION: Everybody loves Janet.
   A. The facts prove the conclusion.
   B. The facts disprove the conclusion.
   C. The facts neither prove nor disprove the conclusion.

4. FACTS: Most of the Torres family lives in East Los Angeles. Many people in East Los Angeles celebrate Cinco de Mayo. Joe is a member of the Torres family.

   CONCLUSION: Joe lives in East Los Angeles.
   A. The facts prove the conclusion.
   B. The facts disprove the conclusion.
   C. The facts neither prove nor disprove the conclusion.

   4._____

5. FACTS: Five professionals each occupy one story of a five-story office building. Dr. Kane's office is above Dr. Assad's. Dr. Johnson's office is between Dr. Kane's and Dr. Conlon's. Dr. Steen's office is between Dr. Conlon's and Dr. Assad's. Dr. Johnson is on the fourth story.

   CONCLUSION: Dr. Kane occupies the top story.
   A. The facts prove the conclusion.
   B. The facts disprove the conclusion.
   C. The facts neither prove nor disprove the conclusion.

   5._____

6. FACTS: To be eligible for membership in the Yukon Society, a person must be able to either tunnel through a snowbank while wearing only a T-shirt and short, or hold his breath for two minutes under water that is 50°F. Ray can only hold his breath for a minute and a half.

   CONCLUSION: Ray can still become a member of the Yukon Society by tunneling through a snowbank while wearing a T-shirt and shorts.
   A. The facts prove the conclusion.
   B. The facts disprove the conclusion.
   C. The facts neither prove nor disprove the conclusion.

   6._____

7. FACTS: A mark is worth five plunks. You can exchange four sharps for a tinplot. It takes eight marks to buy a sharp.

   CONCLUSION: A sharp is the most valuable.
   A. The facts prove the conclusion.
   B. The facts disprove the conclusion.
   C. The facts neither prove nor disprove the conclusion.

   7._____

8. FACTS: There are gibbons, as well as lemurs, who like to play in the trees at the monkey house. All those who like to play in the trees at the monkey house are fed lettuce and bananas.

   CONCLUSION: Lemurs and gibbons are types of monkeys.
   A. The facts prove the conclusion.
   B. The facts disprove the conclusion.
   C. The facts neither prove nor disprove the conclusion.

   8._____

9. **FACTS:** None of the Blackfoot tribes is a Salishan Indian tribe. Salishan Indians came from the northern Pacific Coast. All Salishan Indians live each of the Continental Divide.

9._____

CONCLUSION: No Blackfoot tribes live east of the Continental Divide.
   A. The facts prove the conclusion.
   B. The facts disprove the conclusion.
   C. The facts neither prove nor disprove the conclusion.

Questions 10-17.

DIRECTIONS: Questions 10 through 17 are based on the following reading passage. It is not your knowledge of the particular topic that is being tested, but your ability to reason based on what you have read. The passage is likely to detail several proposed courses of action and factors affecting these proposals. The reading passage is followed by a conclusion or outcome based on the facts in the passage, or a description of a decision taken regarding the situation. The conclusion is followed by a number of statements that have a possible connection to the conclusion. For each statement, you are to determine whether:
   A. The statement proves the conclusion.
   B. The statement supports the conclusion but does not prove it.
   C. The statement disproves the conclusion.
   D. The statement weakens the conclusion but does not disprove it.
   E. The statement has no relevance to the conclusion.

Remember that the conclusion after the passage is to be accepted as the outcome of what actually happened, and that you are being asked to evaluate the impact each statement would have had on the conclusion.

PASSAGE:

    On August 12, Beverly Willey reported that she was in the elevator late on the previous evening after leaving her office on the 16th floor of a large office building. In her report, she states that a man got on the elevator at the 11th floor, pulled her off the elevator, assaulted her, and stole her purse. Ms. Willey reported that she had seen the man in the elevators and hallways of the building before. She believes that the man works in the building. Her description of him is as follows: he is tall, unshaven, with wavy brown hair and a scar on his left cheek. He walks with a pronounced limp, often dragging his left foot behind his right.

CONCLUSION: After Beverly Willey makes her report, the police arrest a 43-year-old man, Barton Black, and charge him with her assault.

10. Barton Black is a former Marine who served in Vietnam, where he sustained shrapnel wounds to the left side of his face and suffered nerve damage in his left leg.
    A. The statement proves the conclusion.
    B. The statement supports the conclusion but does not prove it.
    C. The statement disproves the conclusion.
    D. The statement weakens the conclusion but does not disprove it.
    E. The statement has no relevance to the conclusion.

11. When they arrived at his residence to question him, detectives were greeted at the door by Barton Black, who was tall and clean-shaven.
    A. The statement proves the conclusion.
    B. The statement supports the conclusion but does not prove it.
    C. The statement disproves the conclusion.
    D. The statement weakens the conclusion but does not disprove it.
    E. The statement has no relevance to the conclusion.

12. Barton Black was booked into the county jail several days after Beverly Willey's assault.
    A. The statement proves the conclusion.
    B. The statement supports the conclusion but does not prove it.
    C. The statement disproves the conclusion.
    D. The statement weakens the conclusion but does not disprove it.
    E. The statement has no relevance to the conclusion.

13. Upon further investigation, detectives discover that Beverly Willey does not work at the office building.
    A. The statement proves the conclusion.
    B. The statement supports the conclusion but does not prove it.
    C. The statement disproves the conclusion.
    D. The statement weakens the conclusion but does not disprove it.
    E. The statement has no relevance to the conclusion.

14. Upon further investigation, detectives discover that Barton Black does not work at the office building.
    A. The statement proves the conclusion.
    B. The statement supports the conclusion but does not prove it.
    C. The statement disproves the conclusion.
    D. The statement weakens the conclusion but does not disprove it.
    E. The statement has no relevance to the conclusion.

15. In the spring of the following year, Barton Black is convicted of assaulting Beverly Willey on August 11.
    A. The statement proves the conclusion.
    B. The statement supports the conclusion but does not prove it.
    C. The statement disproves the conclusion.
    D. The statement weakens the conclusion but does not disprove it.
    E. The statement has no relevance to the conclusion.

16. During their investigation of the assault, detectives determine that Beverly Willey 16._____
was assaulted on the 12th floor of the office building.
    A. The statement proves the conclusion.
    B. The statement supports the conclusion but does not prove it.
    C. The statement disproves the conclusion.
    D. The statement weakens the conclusion but does not disprove it.
    E. The statement has no relevance to the conclusion.

17. The day after Beverly Willey's assault, Barton Black fled the area and was never 17._____
seen again.
    A. The statement proves the conclusion.
    B. The statement supports the conclusion but does not prove it.
    C. The statement disproves the conclusion.
    D. The statement weakens the conclusion but does not disprove it.
    E. The statement has no relevance to the conclusion.

Questions 18-25.

DIRECTIONS: Questions 18 through 25 each provide four factual statements and a conclusion based on these statements. After reading the entire question, you will decide whether:
    A. The conclusion is proved by statements I-IV;
    B. The conclusion is disproved by statements I-IV.
    C. The facts are not sufficient to prove or disprove the conclusion.

18. FACTUAL STATEMENTS: 18._____
    I. Among five spice jars on the shelf, the sage is to the right of the parsley.
    II. The pepper is to the left of the basil.
    III. The nutmeg is between the sage and the pepper.
    IV. The pepper is the second spice from the left.

    CONCLUSION: The safe is the farthest to the right.
    A. The conclusion is proved by statements I-IV;
    B. The conclusion is disproved by statements I-IV.
    C. The facts are not sufficient to prove or disprove the conclusion.

19. FACTUAL STATEMENTS: 19._____
    I. Gear X rotates in a clockwise direction if Switch C is in the OFF position.
    II. Gear X will rotate in a counter-clockwise direction is Switch C is ON.
    III. If Gear X is rotating in a clockwise direction, then Gear Y will not be rotating at all.
    IV. Switch C is ON.

    CONCLUSION: Gear X is rotating in a counter-clockwise direction.
    A. The conclusion is proved by statements I-IV;
    B. The conclusion is disproved by statements I-IV.
    C. The facts are not sufficient to prove or disprove the conclusion.

6 (#2)

20. FACTUAL STATEMENTS:
    I. Lane will leave for the Toronto meeting today only if Terence, Rourke, and Jackson all file their marketing reports by the end of the work day.
    II. Rourke will file her report on time only if Ganz submits last quarter's data.
    III. If Terence attends the security meeting, he will attend it with Jackson, and they will not file their marketing reports by the end of the work day.

    CONCLUSION: Lane will leave for the Toronto meeting today.
    A. The conclusion is proved by statements I-IV;
    B. The conclusion is disproved by statements I-IV.
    C. The facts are not sufficient to prove or disprove the conclusion.

    20.____

21. FACTUAL STATEMENTS:
    I. Bob is in second place in the Boston Marathon.
    II. Gregory is winning the Boston Marathon.
    III. There are four miles to go in the race, and Bob is gaining on Gregory at the rate of 100 yards every minute.
    IV. There are 1760 yards in a mile and Gregory's usual pace during the Boston Marathon is one mile every six minutes.

    CONCLUSION: Bob wins the Boston Marathon.
    A. The conclusion is proved by statements I-IV;
    B. The conclusion is disproved by statements I-IV.
    C. The facts are not sufficient to prove or disprove the conclusion.

    21.____

22. FACTUAL STATEMENTS:
    I. Four brothers are named Earl, John, Gary, and Pete.
    II. Earl and Pete are unmarried.
    III. John is shorter than the youngest of the four.
    IV. The oldest brother is married, and is also the tallest.

    CONCLUSION: Gary is the oldest brother.
    A. The conclusion is proved by statements I-IV;
    B. The conclusion is disproved by statements I-IV.
    C. The facts are not sufficient to prove or disprove the conclusion.

    22.____

23. FACTUAL STATEMENTS:
    I. Brigade X is ten miles from the demilitarized zone.
    II. If General Woundwort gives the order, Brigade X will advance to the demilitarized zone, but not quickly enough to reach the zone before the conflict begins.
    III. Brigade Y, five miles behind Brigade X, will not advance unless General Woundwort gives the order.
    IV. Brigade Y advances.

    23.____

36

CONCLUSION: Brigade X reaches the demilitarized zone before the conflict begins.
    A. The conclusion is proved by statements I-IV;
    B. The conclusion is disproved by statements I-IV.
    C. The facts are not sufficient to prove or disprove the conclusion.

24. FACTUAL STATEMENTS:
    I. Jerry has decided to take a cab from Fullerton to Elverton.
    II. Chubby Cab charges $5 plus $3 a mile.
    III. Orange Cab charges $7.50 but gives free mileage for the first 5 miles.
    IV. After the first 5 miles, Orange Cab charges $2.50 a mile.

    CONCLUSION: Orange Cab is the cheaper fare from Fullerton to Elverton.
    A. The conclusion is proved by statements I-IV;
    B. The conclusion is disproved by statements I-IV.
    C. The facts are not sufficient to prove or disprove the conclusion.

25. FACTUAL STATEMENTS:
    I. Dan is never in class when his friend Lucy is absent.
    II. Lucy is never absent unless her mother is sick.
    III. If Lucy is in class, Sergio is in class also.
    IV. Sergio is never in class when Dalton is absent.

    CONCLUSION: If Lucy is absent, Dalton may be in class.
    A. The conclusion is proved by statements I-IV;
    B. The conclusion is disproved by statements I-IV.
    C. The facts are not sufficient to prove or disprove the conclusion.

KEY (CORRECT ANSWERS)

1.	C		11.	E
2.	B		12.	B
3.	B		13.	D
4.	C		14.	E
5.	A		15.	A
6.	A		16.	E
7.	B		17.	C
8.	C		18.	B
9.	C		19.	A
10.	B		20.	C

21.	C
22.	A
23.	B
24.	A
25.	B

9 (#2)

SOLUTIONS TO PROBLEMS

1. CORRECT ANSWER: C
   Statement 1 only tells us that some employees who work in the Testing Department are statisticians. This means that we need to allow the possibility that at least one person in this department is not a statistician. Thus, if a person works in the Testing Department, we cannot conclude whether or not this individual is a statistician.

2. CORRECT ANSWER: B
   If Hank had six coins, then the total of Gail's collection and Lawrence's collection would be four. Thus, if Gail gave all her coins to Lawrence, Lawrence would only have four coins. Thus, it would be impossible for Lawrence to have more coins than Hank.

3. CORRECT ANSWER: B
   Statement 1 tells us that nobody loves everybody. If everybody loved Janet, then Statement 3 would imply that Ken loves everybody. This would contradict statement 1. The conclusion is disproved.

4. CORRECT ANSWER: C
   Although most of the Torres family lives in East Los Angeles, we can assume that some members of this family do not live in East Los Angeles. Thus, we cannot prove or disprove that Joe, who is a member of the Torres family, lives in East Los Angeles.

5. CORRECT ANSWER: A
   Since Dr. Johnson is on the 4th floor, either (a) Dr. Kane is on the 5th floor and Dr. Conlon is on the 3rd floor, or (b) Dr. Kane is on the 3rd floor and Dr. Conlon is on the 5th floor. If option (b) were correct, then since Dr. Assad would be on the 1st floor, it would be impossible for Dr. Steen's office to be between Dr. Conlon and Dr. Assad's office. Therefore, Dr. Kane's office must be on the 5th floor. The order of the doctors' offices, from 5th floor down to the 1st floor is: Dr. Kane, Dr. Johnson, Dr. Conlon, Dr. Steen, Dr. Assad.

6. CORRECT ANSWER: A
   Ray does not satisfy the requirement of holding his breath for two minutes under water, since he can only hold is breath for one minute in that setting. But if he tunnels through a snowbank with just a T-shirt and shorts, he will satisfy the eligibility requirement. Note that the eligibility requirement contains the key word "or." So only one of the two clauses separated by "or" need to be fulfilled.

7. CORRECT ANSWER: B
   Statement 2 says that four sharps is equivalent to one tinplot. This means that a tinplot is worth more than a sharp. The conclusion is disproved. We note that the order of these items, from most valuable to least valuable are: tinplot, sharp, mark, plunk.

8. CORRECT ANSWER: C
   We can only conclude that gibbons and lemurs are fed lettuce and bananas. We can neither prove nor disprove that these animals are types of monkeys.

9. **CORRECT ANSWER: C**
We know that all Salishan Indians live east of the Continental Divide. But some non-members of this tribe of Indians may also live east of the Continental Divide. Since none of the members of the Blackfoot tribe belong to the Salishan Indian tribe, we cannot draw any conclusion about the location of the Blackfoot tribe with respect to the Continental Divide.

18. **CORRECT ANSWER: B**
Since the pepper is second from the left and the nutmeg is between the sage and the pepper, the positions 2, 3, and 4 (from the left) are pepper, nutmeg, sage. By statement II, the basil must be in position 5, which implies that the parsley is in position 1. Therefore, the basil, not the sage, is farthest to the right. The conclusion disproved.

19. **CORRECT ANSWER: A**
Statement II assures us that if switch C is ON, then Gear X is rotating in a counterclockwise direction. The conclusion is proved.

20. **CORRECT ANSWER: C**
Based on Statement IV, followed by Statement II, we conclude that Ganz and Rourke will file their reports on time. Statement III reveals that if Terence and Jackson attend the security meeting, they will fail to file their reports on time. We have no further information if Terence and Jackson attended the security meeting, so we are not able to either confirm or deny that their reports were filed on time. This implies that we cannot know for certain that Lane will leave for his meeting in Toronto.

21. **CORRECT ANSWER: C**
Although Bob is in second place behind Gregory, we cannot deduce how far behind Gregory he is running. At Gregory's current pace, he will cover four miles in 24 minutes. If Bob were only 100 yards behind Gregory, he would catch up to Gregory in one minute. But if Bob were very far behind Gregory, for example 5 miles, this is the equivalent of (5)(1760) = 8800 yards. Then Bob would need 8800/100 = 88 minutes to catch up to Gregory. Thus, the given facts are not sufficient to draw a conclusion.

22. **CORRECT ANSWER: A**
Statement II tells us that neither Earl nor Pete could be the oldest; also, either John or Gary is married. Statement IV reveals that the oldest brother is both married and the tallest. By Statement III, John cannot be the tallest. Since John is not the tallest, he is not the oldest. Thus, the oldest brother must be Gary. The conclusion is proved.

23. **CORRECT ANSWER: B**
By Statements III and IV, General Woundwort must have given the order to advance. Statement II then tells us that Brigade X will advance to the demilitarized zone, but not soon enough before the conflict begins. Thus, the conclusion is disproved.

11 (#2)

24. CORRECT ANSWER: A
If the distance is 5 miles or less, then the cost for the Orange Cab is only $7.50, whereas the cost for the Chubby Cab is $5 + 3x, where x represents the number of miles traveled. For 1 to 5 miles, the cost of the Chubby Cab is between $8 and $20. This means that for a distance of 5 miles, the Orange Cab costs $7.50, whereas the Chubby Cab costs $20. After 5 miles, the cost per mile of the Chubby Cab exceeds the cost per mile of the Orange Cab. Thus, regardless of the actual distance between Fullerton and Elverton, the cost for the Orange Cab will be cheaper than that of the Chubby Cab.

25. CORRECT ANSWER: B
It looks like "Dalton" should be replaced by "Dan" in the conclusion. Then by statement I, if Lucy is absent, Dan is never in class. Thus, the conclusion is disproved.

EVALUATING CONCLUSIONS IN LIGHT OF KNOWN FACTS
EXAMINATION SECTION
TEST 1

DIRECTIONS: Each question or incomplete statement is followed by several suggested answers or completions. Select the one that BEST answers the question or completes the statement. *PRINT THE LETTER OF THE CORRECT ANSWER IN THE SPACE AT THE RIGHT.*

Questions 1-9.

DIRECTIONS: In Questions 1 through 9, you will read a set of facts and a conclusion drawn from them. The conclusion may be valid or invalid, based on the facts. It is your task to determine the validity of the conclusion.
For each question, select the letter before the statement that BEST expresses the relationship between the given facts and the conclusion that has been drawn from them. Your choices are:
    A. The facts prove the conclusion.
    B. The facts disprove the conclusion; or
    C. The facts neither prove nor disprove the conclusion.

1. FACTS: Lauren must use Highway 29 to get to work. Lauren has a meeting today at 9:00 A.M. If she misses the meeting, Lauren will probably lose a major account. Highway 29 is closed all day today for repairs.

   CONCLUSION: Lauren will not be able to get to work.

   A. The facts prove the conclusion.
   B. The facts disprove the conclusion.
   C. The facts neither prove nor disprove the conclusion.

1.____

2. FACTS: The Tumbleweed Follies, a traveling burlesque show, is looking for a new line dancer. The position requires both singing and dancing skills. If the show cannot fill the position by Friday, it will begin to look for a magician to fill the time slot currently held by the line dancers. Willa, who wants to audition for the line dancing position, can sing, but cannot dance.

   CONCLUSION: Willa is qualified to audition for the part of line dancer.

   A. The facts prove the conclusion.
   B. The facts disprove the conclusion.
   C. The facts neither prove nor disprove the conclusion.

2.____

2 (#1)

3. FACTS: Terry owns two dogs, Spike and Stan. One of the dogs is short-haired and has blue eyes. One dog as a pink nose. The blue-eyed dog never barks. One of the dogs has white fur on its paws. Sam has long hair.

   CONCLUSION: Spike never barks.

   A. The facts prove the conclusion.
   B. The facts disprove the conclusion.
   C. The facts neither prove nor disprove the conclusion.

   3.____

4. FACTS: No science teachers are members of the PTA. Some English teachers are members of the PTA. Some English teachers in the PTA also wear glasses. Every PTA member is required to sit on the dunking stool at the student carnival except for those who wear glasses, who will be exempt. Those who are exempt, however, will have to officiate the hamster races. All of the English teachers in the PTA who do not wear glasses are married.

   CONCLUSION: All the married English teachers in the PTA will set on the dunking stool at the student carnival.

   A. The facts prove the conclusion.
   B. The facts disprove the conclusion.
   C. The facts neither prove nor disprove the conclusion.

   4.____

5. FACTS: If the price of fuel is increased and sales remain constant, oil company profits will increase. The price of fuel was increased, and market experts project that sales levels are likely to be maintained.

   CONCLUSION: The price of fuel will increase.

   A. The facts prove the conclusion.
   B. The facts disprove the conclusion.
   C. The facts neither prove nor disprove the conclusion.

   5.____

6. FACTS: Some members of the gymnastics team are double-jointed, and some members of the gymnastics team ae also on the lacrosse team. Some double-jointed members of the gymnastics team are also coaches. All gymnastics team members perform floor exercises, except the coaches. All the double-jointed members of the gymnastics team who are not coaches are freshmen.

   CONCLUSION: Some double-jointed freshmen are coaches.

   A. The facts prove the conclusion.
   B. The facts disprove the conclusion.
   C. The facts neither prove nor disprove the conclusion.

   6.____

7. FACTS: Each member of the International Society speaks at least one foreign language, but no member speaks more than four foreign languages. Five members speak Spanish; three speak Mandarin; four speak French; four speak German; and five speak a foreign language other than Spanish, Mandarin, French, or German.

   CONCLUSION: The lowest possible number of members in the International Society is eight.

   A. The facts prove the conclusion.
   B. The facts disprove the conclusion.
   C. The facts neither prove nor disprove the conclusion.

   7._____

8. FACTS: Mary keeps seven cats in her apartment. Only three of the cats will eat the same kind of food. Mary wants to keep at least one extra bag of each kind of food.

   CONCLUSION: The minimum number of bags Mary will need to keep as extra is 7.

   A. The facts prove the conclusion.
   B. The facts disprove the conclusion.
   C. The facts neither prove nor disprove the conclusion.

   8._____

9. FACTS: In Ed and Marie's exercise group, everyone likes the treadmill or the stationary bicycle, or both, but Ed does not like the stationary bicycle. Marie has not expressed a preference, but spends most of her time on the stationary bicycle.

   CONCLUSION: Everyone in the group who does not like the treadmill likes the stationary bicycle.

   A. The facts prove the conclusion.
   B. The facts disprove the conclusion.
   C. The facts neither prove nor disprove the conclusion.

   9._____

Questions 10-17.

DIRECTIONS: Questions 10 through 17 are based on the following reading passage. It is not your knowledge of the particular topic that is being tested, but your ability to reason based on what you have read. The passage is likely to detail several proposed courses of action and factors affecting these proposals. The reading passage is followed by a conclusion or outcome based on the facts in the passage, or a description of a decision taken regarding the situation. The conclusion is followed by a number of statements that have a possible connection to the conclusion. For each statement, you are to determine whether:

A. The statement proves the conclusion.
B. The statement supports the conclusion but does not prove it.
C. The statement disproves the conclusion.
D. The statement weakens the conclusion but does not disprove it.
E. The statement has no relevance to the conclusion.

Remember that the conclusion after the passage is to be accepted as the outcome of what actually happened, and that you are being asked to evaluate the impact each statement would have had on the conclusion.

PASSAGE

The Owyhee Mission School District's Board of Directors is hosting a public meeting to debate the merits of the proposed abolition of all bilingual education programs within the district. The group that has made the proposal believes the programs, which teach immigrant children academic subjects in their native language until they have learned English well enough to join mainstream classes, inhibit the ability of students to acquire English quickly and succeed in school and in the larger American society. Such programs, they argue, are also a wasteful drain on the district's already scant resources.

At the meeting, several teachers and parents stand to speak out against the proposal. The purpose of an education, they say, should be to build upon, rather than dismantle, a minority child's language and culture. By teaching children in academic subjects in their native tongues, while simultaneously offering English language instruction, schools can meet the goals of learning English and progressing through academic subjects along with their peers.

Hiram Nguyen, a representative of the parents whose children are currently enrolled in bilingual education, stands at the meeting to express the parents' wishes. The parents have been polled, he says, and are overwhelmingly of the opinion that while language and culture are important to them, they are not things that will disappear from the students' lives if they are no longer taught in the classroom. The most important issue for the parents is whether their children will succeed in school and be competitive in the larger American society. If bilingual education can be demonstrated to do that, then the parents are in favor of continuing it.

At the end of the meeting, a proponent of the plan, Oscar Ramos, stands to clarify some misconceptions about the proposal. It does not call for a "sink or swim" approach, he says, but allows for an interpreter to be present in mainstream classes to explain anything a student finds too complex or confusing.

The last word of the meeting is given to Delia Cruz, a bilingual teacher at one of the district's elementary schools. A student is bound to find anything complex or confusing, she says, if it is spoken in a language he has never heard before. It is more wasteful to place children in classrooms where they don't understand anything, she says, than it is to try to teach them something useful as they are learning the English language.

CONCLUSION: After the meeting, the Owyhee Mission School District's Board of Directors votes to terminate all the district's bilingual education programs at the end of the current academic year, but to maintain the current level of funding to each of the schools that have programs cut.

10. A poll conducted by the *Los Angeles Times* at approximately the same time as the Board's meeting indicated that 75% of the people were opposed to bilingual education; among Latinos, opposition was 84%.
    A. The statement proves the conclusion.
    B. The statement supports the conclusion but does not prove it.
    C. The statement disproves the conclusion.
    D. The statement weakens the conclusion but does not disprove it.
    E. The statement has no relevance to the conclusion.

10.____

11. Of all the studies connected on bilingual education programs, 64% indicate that students learned English grammar better in "sink or swim" classes without any special features than they did in bilingual education classes.
    A. The statement proves the conclusion.
    B. The statement supports the conclusion but does not prove it.
    C. The statement disproves the conclusion.
    D. The statement weakens the conclusion but does not disprove it.
    E. The statement has no relevance to the conclusion.

11.____

12. In the academic year that begins after the Board's vote, Montgomery Burns Elementary, an Owyhee Mission District school, launches a new bilingual program for the children of Somali immigrants.
    A. The statement proves the conclusion.
    B. The statement supports the conclusion but does not prove it.
    C. The statement disproves the conclusion.
    D. The statement weakens the conclusion but does not disprove it.
    E. The statement has no relevance to the conclusion.

12.____

13. In the previous academic year, under severe budget restraints, the Owyhee Mission District cut all physical education, music, and art classes, but its funding for bilingual education classes increased by 18%.
    A. The statement proves the conclusion.
    B. The statement supports the conclusion but does not prove it.
    C. The statement disproves the conclusion.
    D. The statement weakens the conclusion but does not disprove it.
    E. The statement has no relevance to the conclusion.

13.____

14. Before the Board votes, a polling consultant conducts randomly sampled assessments of immigrant students who enrolled in Owyhee District schools at a time when they did not speak any English at all. Ten years after graduating from high school, 44% of those who received bilingual education were professionals – doctors, lawyers, educators, engineers, etc. Of those who did not receive bilingual education, 38% were professionals.
    A. The statement proves the conclusion.
    B. The statement supports the conclusion but does not prove it.
    C. The statement disproves the conclusion.
    D. The statement weakens the conclusion but does not disprove it.
    E. The statement has no relevance to the conclusion.

14.____

15. Over the past several years, the scores of Owyhee District students have gradually declined, and enrollment numbers have followed as anxious parents transferred their children to other schools or applied for a state-funded voucher program.
    A. The statement proves the conclusion.
    B. The statement supports the conclusion but does not prove it.
    C. The statement disproves the conclusion.
    D. The statement weakens the conclusion but does not disprove it.
    E. The statement has no relevance to the conclusion.

15._____

16. California and Massachusetts, two of the most liberal states in the country, have each passed ballot measures banning bilingual education in public schools.
    A. The statement proves the conclusion.
    B. The statement supports the conclusion but does not prove it.
    C. The statement disproves the conclusion.
    D. The statement weakens the conclusion but does not disprove it.
    E. The statement has no relevance to the conclusion.

16._____

17. In the academic year that begins after the Board's vote, no Owyhee Mission Schools are conducting bilingual instruction.
    A. The statement proves the conclusion.
    B. The statement supports the conclusion but does not prove it.
    C. The statement disproves the conclusion.
    D. The statement weakens the conclusion but does not disprove it.
    E. The statement has no relevance to the conclusion.

17._____

Questions 18-25.

DIRECTIONS: Questions 18 through 25 each provide four factual statements and a conclusion based on these statements. After reading the entire question, you will decide whether:
    A. The conclusion is proved by Statements 1-4;
    B. The conclusion is disproved by Statements 1-4;
    C. The facts are not sufficient to prove or disprove the conclusion.

18. FACTUAL STATEMENTS:
    1) Gear X rotates in a clockwise direction if Switch C is in the OFF position.
    2) Gear X will rotate in a counter-clockwise direction if Switch C is ON.
    3) If Gear X is rotating in a clockwise direction, then Gear Y will not be rotating at all.
    4) Switch C is OFF.

    CONCLUSION: Gear Y is rotating.

    A. The conclusion is proved by Statements 1-4;
    B. The conclusion is disproved by Statements 1-4;
    C. The facts are not sufficient to prove or disprove the conclusion.

18._____

7 (#1)

19. FACTUAL STATEMENTS:
    1) Mark is older than Jim but younger than Dan.
    2) Fern is older than Mark but younger than Silas.
    3) Dan is younger than Silas but older than Edward.
    4) Edward is older than Mark but younger than Fern.

    CONCLUSION: Dan is older than Fern.

    A. The conclusion is proved by Statements 1-4;
    B. The conclusion is disproved by Statements 1-4;
    C. The facts are not sufficient to prove or disprove the conclusion.

    19.____

20. FACTUAL STATEMENTS:
    1) Each of Fred's three sofa cushions lies on top of four lost coins.
    2) The cushion on the right covers two pennies and two dimes.
    3) The middle cushion covers two dimes and two quarters.
    4) The cushion on the left covers two nickels and two quarters.

    CONCLUSION: To be guaranteed of retrieving at least one coin of each denomination, and without looking at any of the coins, Frank must take three coins each from under the cushions on the right and the left.

    A. The conclusion is proved by Statements 1-4;
    B. The conclusion is disproved by Statements 1-4;
    C. The facts are not sufficient to prove or disprove the conclusion.

    20.____

21. FACTUAL STATEMENTS:
    1) The door to the hammer mill chamber is locked if light 6 is red.
    2) The door to the hammer mill chamber is locked only when the mill is operating.
    3) If the mill is not operating, light 6 is blue.
    4) The door to the hammer mill chamber is locked.

    CONCLUSION: The mill is in operation.

    A. The conclusion is proved by Statements 1-4;
    B. The conclusion is disproved by Statements 1-4;
    C. The facts are not sufficient to prove or disprove the conclusion.

    21.____

22. FACTUAL STATEMENTS:
    1) In a five-story office building, where each story is occupied by a single professional, Dr. Kane's office is above Dr. Assad's.
    2) Dr. Johnson's office is between Dr. Kane's and Dr. Conlon's.
    3) Dr. Steen's office is between Dr. Conlon's and Dr. Assad's.
    4) Dr. Johnson is on the fourth story.

    CONCLUSION: Dr. Steen occupies the second story.

    22.____

A. The conclusion is proved by Statements 1-4;
B. The conclusion is disproved by Statements 1-4;
C. The facts are not sufficient to prove or disprove the conclusion.

23. FACTUAL STATEMENTS:
    1) On Saturday, farmers Hank, Earl, Roy, and Cletus plowed a total of 520 acres.
    2) Hank plowed twice as many acres as Roy.
    3) Roy plowed half as much as the farmer who plowed the most.
    4) Cletus plowed 160 acres.

    CONCLUSION: Hank plowed 200 acres.
    A. The conclusion is proved by Statements 1-4;
    B. The conclusion is disproved by Statements 1-4;
    C. The facts are not sufficient to prove or disprove the conclusion.

24. FACTUAL STATEMENTS:
    1) Four travelers – Tina, Jodie, Alex, and Oscar – each traveled to a different island – Aruba, Jamaica, Nevis, and Barbados – but not necessarily respectively.
    2) Tina did not travel as far to Jamaica as Jodie traveled to her island.
    3) Oscar traveled twice as far as Alex, who traveled the same distance as the traveler who went to Aruba.
    4) Oscar went to Barbados.

    CONCLUSION: Oscar traveled the farthest.

    A. The conclusion is proved by Statements 1-4;
    B. The conclusion is disproved by Statements 1-4;
    C. The facts are not sufficient to prove or disprove the conclusion.

25. FACTUAL STATEMENT:
    1) In the natural history museum, every Native American display that contains pottery also contains beadwork.
    2) Some of the displays containing lodge replicas also contain beadwork.
    3) The display on the Choctaw, a Native American tribe, contains pottery.
    4) The display on the Modoc, a Native American tribe, contains only two of these items.

    CONCLUSION: If the Modoc display contains pottery, it does not contain lodge replicas.

    A. The conclusion is proved by Statements 1-4;
    B. The conclusion is disproved by Statements 1-4;
    C. The facts are not sufficient to prove or disprove the conclusion.

KEY (CORRECT ANSWERS)

1.	A		11.	B
2.	B		12.	C
3.	A		13.	B
4.	A		14.	D
5.	C		15.	E
6.	B		16.	E
7.	B		17.	A
8.	B		18.	B
9.	A		19.	C
10.	B		20.	A

21. A
22. A
23. C
24. A
25. A

TEST 2

DIRECTIONS: Each question or incomplete statement is followed by several suggested answers or completions. Select the one that BEST answers the question or completes the statement. *PRINT THE LETTER OF THE CORRECT ANSWER IN THE SPACE AT THE RIGHT.*

Questions 1-9.

DIRECTIONS: In Questions 1 through 9, you will read a set of facts and a conclusion drawn from them. The conclusion may be valid or invalid, based on the facts. It is your task to determine the validity of the conclusion.
For each question, select the letter before the statement that BEST expresses the relationship between the given facts and the conclusion that has been drawn from them. Your choices are:
    A. The facts prove the conclusion.
    B. The facts disprove the conclusion; or
    C. The facts neither prove nor disprove the conclusion.

1. FACTS: If the maximum allowable income for Medicaid recipients is increased, the number of Medicaid recipients will increase. If the number of Medicaid recipients increases, more funds must be allocated to the Medicaid program, which will require a tax increase. Taxes cannot be approved without the approval of the legislature. The legislature probably will not approve a tax increase.

    CONCLUSION: The maximum allowable income for Medicaid recipients will increase.

    A. The facts prove the conclusion.
    B. The facts disprove the conclusion; or
    C. The facts neither prove nor disprove the conclusion.

1.____

2. FACTS: All the dentists on the baseball team are short. Everyone in the dugout is a dentist, but not everyone in the dugout is short. The baseball team is not made up of people of any particular profession.

    CONCLUSION: Some people who are not dentists are in the dugout.

    A. The facts prove the conclusion.
    B. The facts disprove the conclusion; or
    C. The facts neither prove nor disprove the conclusion.

2.____

3. FACTS: A taxi company's fleet is divided into two fleets. Fleet One contains cabs A, B, C, and D. Fleet Two contains E, F, G, and H. Each cab is either yellow or green. Five of the cabs are yellow. Cabs A and E are not both yellow. Either Cab C or F, or both, are not yellow. Cabs B and H are either both yellow or both green.

    CONCLUSION: Cab H is green.

3.____

52

2 (#2)

   A. The facts prove the conclusion.
   B. The facts disprove the conclusion; or
   C. The facts neither prove nor disprove the conclusion.

4. FACTS: Most people in the skydiving club are not afraid of heights. Everyone in the skydiving club makes three parachute jumps a month.

   CONCLUSION: At least one person who is afraid of heights makes three parachute jumps a month.

   A. The facts prove the conclusion.
   B. The facts disprove the conclusion; or
   C. The facts neither prove nor disprove the conclusion.

4.____

5. FACTS: If the Board approves the new rule, the agency will move to a new location immediately. If the agency moves, five new supervisors will be immediately appointed. The Board has approved the new proposal.

   CONCLUSION: No new supervisors were appointed.

   A. The facts prove the conclusion.
   B. The facts disprove the conclusion; or
   C. The facts neither prove nor disprove the conclusion.

5.____

6. FACTS: All the workers at the supermarket chew gum when they sack groceries. Sometimes Lance, a supermarket worker, doesn't chew gum at all when he works. Another supermarket worker, Jenny, chews gum the whole time she is at work.

   CONCLUSION: Jenny always sacks groceries when she is at work.

6.____

7. FACTS: Lake Lottawatta is bigger than Lake Tacomi. Lake Tacomi and Lake Ottawa are exactly the same size. All lakes in Montana are bigger than Lake Ottawa.

   CONCLUSION: Lake Lottawatta is in Montana.

   A. The facts prove the conclusion.
   B. The facts disprove the conclusion; or
   C. The facts neither prove nor disprove the conclusion.

7.____

8. FACTS: Two men, Cox and Taylor, are playing poker at a table. Taylor has a pair of aces in his hand. One man is smoking a cigar. One of them has no pairs in his hand and is wearing an eye patch. The man wearing the eye patch is smoking a cigar. One man is bald.

   CONCLUSION: Cox is smoking a cigar.

8.____

A. The facts prove the conclusion.
B. The facts disprove the conclusion; or
C. The facts neither prove nor disprove the conclusion.

9. FACTS: All Kwakiutls are Wakashan Indians. All Wakashan Indians originated on Vancouver Island. The Nootka also originated on Vancouver Island. 9.____

   CONCLUSION: Kwakiutls originated on Vancouver Island.

   A. The facts prove the conclusion.
   B. The facts disprove the conclusion; or
   C. The facts neither prove nor disprove the conclusion.

Questions 10-17.

DIRECTIONS: Questions 10 through 17 are based on the following reading passage. It is not your knowledge of the particular topic that is being tested, but your ability to reason based on what you have read. The passage is likely to detail several proposed courses of action and factors affecting these proposals. The reading passage is followed by a conclusion or outcome based on the facts in the passage, or a description of a decision taken regarding the situation. The conclusion is followed by a number of statements that have a possible connection to the conclusion. For each statement, you are to determine whether:
A. The statement proves the conclusion.
B. The statement supports the conclusion but does not prove it.
C. The statement disproves the conclusion.
D. The statement weakens the conclusion but does not disprove it.
E. The statement has no relevance to the conclusion.

Remember that the conclusion after the passage is to be accepted as the outcome of what actually happened, and that you are being asked to evaluate the impact each statement would have had on the conclusion.

PASSAGE

The World Wide Web portal and search engine, HipBot, is considering becoming a subscription-only service, locking out nonsubscribers from the content on its web site. HipBot currently relies solely on advertising revenues.

HipBot's content director says that by taking in an annual fee from each customer, the company can both increase profits and provide premium content that no other portal can match.

The marketing director disagrees, saying that there is no guarantee that anyone who now visits the web site for free will agree to pay for the privilege of visiting it again. Most will probably simply use the other major portals. Also, HipBot's advertising clients will not be happy when they learn that the site will be viewed by a more limited number of people.

4 (#2)

CONCLUSION: In January of 2016, the CEO of HipBot decides to keep the portal open to all web users, with some limited "premium content" available to subscribers who don't mind paying a little extra to access it. The company will aim to maintain, or perhaps increase, its advertising revenue.

10. In an independent marketing survey, 62% of respondents said they "strongly agree" with the following statement: "I almost never pay attention to advertisements that appear on the World Wide Web." 10._____
    A. The statement proves the conclusion.
    B. The statement supports the conclusion but does not prove it.
    C. The statement disproves the conclusion.
    D. The statement weakens the conclusion but does not disprove it.
    E. The statement has no relevance to the conclusion.

11. When it learns about the subscription-only debate going on at HipBot, Wernham Hogg Entertainment, one of HipBot's most reliable clients, says it will withdraw its ads and place them on a free web portal if HipBot decides to limit its content to subscribers. Wernham Hogg pays HipBot about $6 million annually – about 12% of HipBot's gross revenues – to run its ads online. 11._____
    A. The statement proves the conclusion.
    B. The statement supports the conclusion but does not prove it.
    C. The statement disproves the conclusion.
    D. The statement weakens the conclusion but does not disprove it.
    E. The statement has no relevance to the conclusion.

12. At the end of the second quarter of FY 2016, after continued stagnant profits, the CEO of HipBot assembles a blue ribbon commission to gather and analyze data on the costs, benefits, and feasibility of adding a limited amount of "premium" content to the HipBot portal. 12._____
    A. The statement proves the conclusion.
    B. The statement supports the conclusion but does not prove it.
    C. The statement disproves the conclusion.
    D. The statement weakens the conclusion but does not disprove it.
    E. The statement has no relevance to the conclusion.

13. In the following fiscal year, Wernham Hogg Entertainment, satisfied with the "hit counts" on HipBot's free web site, spends another $1 million on advertisements that will appear on web pages that are available to HipBot's "premium subscribers. 13._____
    A. The statement proves the conclusion.
    B. The statement supports the conclusion but does not prove it.
    C. The statement disproves the conclusion.
    D. The statement weakens the conclusion but does not disprove it.
    E. The statement has no relevance to the conclusion.

14. HipBot's information technology director reports that the engineers in his department have come up with a feature that will search not only individual web pages, but tie into other web-based search engines, as well, and then comb through all these results to find those most relevant to the user's search. 14._____

5 (#2)

    A. The statement proves the conclusion.
    B. The statement supports the conclusion but does not prove it.
    C. The statement disproves the conclusion.
    D. The statement weakens the conclusion but does not disprove it.
    E. The statement has no relevance to the conclusion.

15. In an independent marketing survey, 79% of respondents said they "strongly agree" with the following statement: "Many web sites are so dominated by advertisements these days that it is increasingly frustrating to find the content I want to read or see." 15.____
    A. The statement proves the conclusion.
    B. The statement supports the conclusion but does not prove it.
    C. The statement disproves the conclusion.
    D. The statement weakens the conclusion but does not disprove it.
    E. The statement has no relevance to the conclusion.

16. After three years of studies at the federal level, the Department of Commerce releases a report suggesting that, in general, the only private "subscriber-only" web sites that do well financially are those with a very specialized user population. 16.____
    A. The statement proves the conclusion.
    B. The statement supports the conclusion but does not prove it.
    C. The statement disproves the conclusion.
    D. The statement weakens the conclusion but does not disprove it.
    E. The statement has no relevance to the conclusion.

17. HipBot's own marketing research indicates that the introduction of premium content has the potential to attract new users to the HipBot portal. 17.____
    A. The statement proves the conclusion.
    B. The statement supports the conclusion but does not prove it.
    C. The statement disproves the conclusion.
    D. The statement weakens the conclusion but does not disprove it.
    E. The statement has no relevance to the conclusion.

Questions 18-25.

DIRECTIONS: Questions 18 through 25 each provide four factual statements and a conclusion based on these statements. After reading the entire question, you will decide whether:
    A. The conclusion is proved by Statements 1-4;
    B. The conclusion is disproved by Statements 1-4;
    C. The facts are not sufficient to prove or disprove the conclusion.

18. FACTUAL STATEMENTS:
   1) If the alarm goes off, Sam will wake up.
   2) If Tandy wakes up before 4:00, Linda will leave the bedroom and sleep on the couch.
   3) If Linda leaves the bedroom, she'll check the alarm to make sure it is working.
   4) The alarm goes off.

   CONCLUSION: Tandy woke up before 4:00.

   A. The conclusion is proved by Statements 1-4;
   B. The conclusion is disproved by Statements 1-4;
   C. The facts are not sufficient to prove or disprove the conclusion.

19. FACTUAL STATEMENTS:
   1) Four brothers are named Earl, John, Gary, and Pete.
   2) Earl and Pete are unmarried.
   3) John is shorter than the youngest of the four.
   4) The oldest brother is married, and is also the tallest.

   CONCLUSION: Pete is the youngest brother.

   A. The conclusion is proved by Statements 1-4;
   B. The conclusion is disproved by Statements 1-4;
   C. The facts are not sufficient to prove or disprove the conclusion.

20. FACTUAL STATEMENTS:
   1) Automobile engines are cooled either by air or by liquid.
   2) If the engine is small and simple enough, air from a belt-driven fan will cool it sufficiently.
   3) Most newer automobile engines are too complicated to be air-cooled.
   4) Air-cooled engines are cheaper and easier to build then liquid-cooled engines.

   CONCLUSION: Most newer automobile engines use liquid coolant.

   A. The conclusion is proved by Statements 1-4;
   B. The conclusion is disproved by Statements 1-4;
   C. The facts are not sufficient to prove or disprove the conclusion.

21. FACTUAL STATEMENTS:
   1) Erica will only file a lawsuit if she is injured while parasailing.
   2) If Rick orders Trip to run a rope test, Trip will check the rigging.
   3) If the rigging does not malfunction, Erica will not be injured.
   4) Rick orders Trip to run a rope test.

CONCLUSION: Erica does not file a lawsuit.

   A. The conclusion is proved by Statements 1-4;
   B. The conclusion is disproved by Statements 1-4;
   C. The facts are not sufficient to prove or disprove the conclusion.

22. FACTUAL STATEMENTS:
   1) On Maple Street, which is four blocks long, Bill's shop is two blocks east of Ken's shop.
   2) Ken's shop is one block west of the only shop on Maple Street with an awning.
   3) Erma's shop is one block west of the easternmost block.
   4) Bill's shop is on the easternmost block.

   CONCLUSION: Bill's shop has an awning.

   A. The conclusion is proved by Statements 1-4;
   B. The conclusion is disproved by Statements 1-4;
   C. The facts are not sufficient to prove or disprove the conclusion.

23. FACTUAL STATEMENTS:
   1) Gear X rotates in a clockwise direction if Switch C is in the OFF position.
   2) Gear X will rotate in a counter-clockwise direction if Switch C is ON.
   3) If Gear X is rotating in a clockwise direction, then Gear Y will not be rotating at all.
   4) Gear Y is rotating.

   CONCLUSION: Gear X is rotating in a counter-clockwise direction.

   A. The conclusion is proved by Statements 1-4;
   B. The conclusion is disproved by Statements 1-4;
   C. The facts are not sufficient to prove or disprove the conclusion.

24. FACTUAL STATEMENTS:
   1) The Republic of Garbanzo's currency system has four basic denominations: the pastor, the noble, the donner, and the rojo.
   2) A pastor is worth 2 nobles.
   3) 2 donners can be exchanged for a rojo.
   4) 3 pastors are equal in value to 2 donners.

   CONCLUSION: The rojo is most valuable.

   A. The conclusion is proved by Statements 1-4;
   B. The conclusion is disproved by Statements 1-4;
   C. The facts are not sufficient to prove or disprove the conclusion.

8 (#2)

25. FACTUAL STATEMENTS: 25._____
    1) At Prickett's Nursery, the only citrus trees left are either Meyer lemons or Valencia oranges, and every citrus tree left is either a dwarf or a semidwarf.
    2) Half of the semidwarf trees are Meyer lemons.
    3) There are more semidwarf trees left than dwarf trees.
    4) A quarter of the dwarf trees are Valencia oranges.

    CONCLUSION: There are more Valencia oranges left at Prickett's Nursery than Meyer lemons.

    A. The conclusion is proved by Statements 1-4;
    B. The conclusion is disproved by Statements 1-4;
    C. The facts are not sufficient to prove or disprove the conclusion.

KEY (CORRECT ANSWERS)

1.	C		11.	B
2.	B		12.	C
3.	B		13.	A
4.	A		14.	E
5.	B		15.	D
6.	C		16.	B
7.	C		17.	B
8.	A		18.	C
9.	A		19.	C
10.	E		20.	A

21. C
22. B
23. C
24. A
25. B

LOGICAL REASONING
EVALUATING CONCLUSIONS IN LIGHT OF KNOWN FACTS
EXAMINATION SECTION
TEST 1

COMMENTARY

This section is designed to provide practice questions in evaluating conclusions when you are given specific data to work with.

We suggest you do the questions three at a time, consulting the answer key and then the solution section for any questions you may have missed. It's a good idea to try the questions again a week before the exam.

In the validity of conclusion type of question, you are first given a reading passage which describes a particular situation. The passage may be on any topic, as it is not your knowledge of the topic that is being tested, but your reasoning abilities. The passage is likely to detail several proposed courses of action and factors affecting these proposals. The reading passage is followed by a conclusion based on the facts in the passage, or a description of a decision taken regarding the situation. The conclusion is followed by a number of statements which have a possible connection to the conclusion. For each statement, you are to determine whether:

- A. The statement proves the conclusion.
- B. The statement supports the conclusion but does not prove it.
- C. The statement disproves the conclusion.
- D. The statement weakens the conclusion but does not disprove it.
- E. The statement has no relevance to the conclusion.

Remember that the conclusion after the passage is to be accepted as the outcome of what actually happened, and that you are being asked to evaluate the impact each statement would have had on the conclusion.

Questions 1-8.

DIRECTIONS: Questions 1 through 8 are based on the following paragraph.

In May of 2018, Mr. Bryan inherited a clothing store on Main Street in a small New England town. The store has specialized in selling quality men's and women's clothing since 1920. Business has been stable throughout the years, neither increasing nor decreasing. He has an opportunity to buy two adjacent stores which would enable him to add a wider range and style of clothing. In order to do this, he would have to borrow a substantial amount of money. He also risks losing the goodwill of his present clientele.

CONCLUSION: On November 7, 2018, Mr. Bryan tells the owner of the two adjacent stores that he has decided not to purchase them. He feels that it would be best to simply maintain his present marketing position, as there would not be enough new business to support an expansion.

A. The statement proves the conclusion.
B. The statement supports the conclusion but does not prove it.
C. The statement disproves the conclusion.
D. The statement weakens the conclusion.
E. The statement is irrelevant to the conclusion.

1. A large new branch of the county's community college holds its first classes in September. 1.____

2. The town's largest factory shuts down with no indication that it will reopen. 2.____

3. The United States Census showed that the number of children per household dropped from 2.4 to 2.1 since the last census. 3.____

4. Mr. Bryan's brother tells him of a new clothing boutique specializing in casual women's clothing which is opening soon. 4.____

5. Mr. Bryan's sister buys her baby several items for Christmas at Mr. Bryan's store. 5.____

6. Mrs. McIntyre, the President of the Town Council, brings Mr. Bryan a home-baked pumpkin pie in honor of his store's 100th anniversary. They discuss the changes that have taken place in the town, and she comments on how his store has maintained the same look and feel over the years. 6.____

7. In October, Mr. Bryan's aunt lends him $50,000. 7.____

8. The Town Council has just announced that the town is eligible for funding from a federal project designed to encourage the location of new businesses in the central districts of cities and towns. 8.____

Questions 9-18.

DIRECTIONS: Questions 9 through 18 are based on the following paragraph.

A proposal was put before the legislative body of a country to require air bags in all automobiles manufactured for domestic use in that country after 2019. The air bag, made of nylon or plastic, is designed to inflate automatically within a car at the impact of a collision, thus protecting front-seat occupants from being thrown forward. There has been much support of the measure from consumer groups, the insurance industry, key legislators, and the general public. The country's automobile manufacturers, who contend the new crash equipment would add up to $1,000 to car prices and provide no more protection than existing seat belts, are against the proposed legislation

CONCLUSION: On April 21, 2014, the legislation requiring air bags in all automobiles manufactured for domestic use in that country after 2019.

A. The statement proves the conclusion.
B. The statement supports the conclusion but does not prove it.
C. The statement disproves the conclusion.
D. The statement weakens the conclusion.
E. The statement is irrelevant to the conclusion.

9. A study has shown that 59% of car occupants do not use seat belts. 9._____

10. The country's Department of Transportation has estimated that the crash protection equipment would save up to 5,900 lives each year. 10._____

11. On April 27, 2013, Augusta Raneoni was named head of an advisory committee to gather and analyze data on the costs, benefits, and feasibility of the proposed legislation on air bags in automobiles. 11._____

12. Consumer groups and the insurance industry accuse the legislature of rejecting passage of the regulation for political reasons. 12._____

13. A study by the Committee on Imports and Exports projected that the sales of imported cars would rise dramatically in 2019 because imported cars do not have to include air bags, and can be sold more cheaply. 13._____

14. Research has shown that air bags, if produced on a large scale, would cost about $200 apiece, and would provide more reliable protection than any other type of seat belt. 14._____

15. Auto sales in 2011 increased 3% over the previous year. 15._____

16. A Department of Transportation report in July of 2020 credits a drop in automobile deaths of 4,100 to the use of air bags. 16._____

17. In June of 2014, the lobbyist of the largest insurance company receives a bonus for her work on the passage of the air bag legislation. 17._____

18. In 2020, the stock in crash protection equipment has risen three-fold over the previous year. 18._____

Questions 19-25.

DIRECTIONS: Questions 19 through 25 are based on the following paragraph.

On a national television talk show, Joan Rivera, a famous comedienne, has recently insulted the physical appearances of a famous actress and the dead wife of an ex-President. There has been a flurry of controversy over her comments, and much discussion of the incident has appeared in the press. Most of the comments have been negative. It appears that this tie she might have gone too far. There have been cancellations of two of her five scheduled performances in the two weeks since the show was televised, and Joan's been receiving a lot of negative mail. Because of the controversy, she has an interview with a national news magazine at the end of the week, and her press agent is strongly urging her to apologize publicly. She feels strongly that her comments were no worse than any other she has ever made, and that the whole incident will *blow over* soon. She respects her press agent's judgment, however, as his assessment of public sentiment tends to be very accurate.

CONCLUSION: Joan does not apologize publicly, and during the interview she challenges the actress to a weight-losing contest. For every pound the actress loses, Joan says she will donate $1 to the Cellulite Prevention League.

A. The statement proves the conclusion.
B. The statement supports the conclusion but does not prove it.
C. The statement disproves the conclusion.
D. The statement weakens the conclusion.
E. The statement is irrelevant to the conclusion.

19. Joan's mother, who she is very fond of, is very upset with Joan's comments. 19.____

20. Six months after the interview, Joan's income has doubled. 20.____

21. Joan's agent is pleased with the way Joan handles the interview. 21.____

22. Joan's sister has been appointed Treasurer of the Cellulite Prevention League 22.____
In her report, she states that Joan's $12 contribution is the only amount that has been donated to the League in its first six months.

23. The magazine receives many letters commending Joan for the courage it 23.____
took for her to apologize publicly in the interview.

24. Immediately after the interview appears, another one of Joan's performances 24.____
is cancelled.

25. Due to a printers' strike, the article was not published until the following week. 25.____

Questions 26-30.

DIRECTIONS: Questions 25 through 30 are based on the following paragraph.

The law-making body of Country X must decide what to do about the issue of recording television shows for home use. There is currently no law against recording shows directly from the TV as long as the DVDs are not used for commercial purposes. The increasing popularity of pay TV and satellite systems, combined with the increasing number of homes that own recording equipment, has caused a great deal of concern in some segments of the entertainment industry. Companies that own the rights to films, popular television shows, and sporting events feel that their copyright privileges are being violated, and they are seeking compensation or the banning of TV recording. Legislation has been introduced to make it illegal to record television programs for home use. Separate proposed legislation is also pending that would continue to allow recording of TV shows for home use, but would place a tax of 10% on each DVD that is purchased for home use. The income from that tax would then be proportionately distributed as royalties to those owning the rights to programs being aired. A weighted point system coupled with the averaging of several national viewing rating systems would be used to determine the royalties. There is a great deal of lobbying being done for both bills, as the manufacturers of DVDs and recording equipment are against the passage of the bills.

CONCLUSION: The legislature of Country X rejects both bills by a wide margin.

- A. The statement proves the conclusion.
  - B. The statement supports the conclusion but does not prove it.
  - C. The statement disproves the conclusion.
  - D. The statement weakens the conclusion.
  - E. The statement is irrelevant to the conclusion.

26. Country X's Department of Taxation hires 500 new employees to handle the increased paperwork created by the new tax on DVDs. 26.____

27. A study conducted by the country's most prestigious accounting firm shows that the cost of implementing the proposed new DVD tax would be greater than the income expected from it. 27.____

28. It is estimated that 80% of all those working in the entertainment industry, excluding performers, own DVD recorders. 28.____

29. The head of Country X's law enforcement agency states that legislation banning the home recording of TV shows would be unenforceable. 29.____

30. Financial experts predict that unless a tax is placed on DVDs, several large companies in the entertainment industry will have to file for bankruptcy. 30.____

Questions 31-38.

DIRECTIONS: Questions 31 through 38 are variations on the type of question you just had. It is important that you read the question very carefully to determine exactly what is required.

31. In this question, select the choice that is MOST relevant to the conclusion. 31.____
    I. The Buffalo Bills football team is in second place in its division.
    II. The New England Patriots are in first place in the same division.
    III. There are two games left to play in the season, and the Bills will not play the Patriots again.
    IV. The New England Patriots won ten games and lost four games, and the Buffalo Bills have won eight games and lost six games.
    CONCLUSION: The Buffalo Bills win their division.
    A. The conclusion is proved by sentences I-IV.
    B. The conclusion is disproved by sentences I-IV.
    C. The facts are not sufficient to prove or disprove the conclusion.

32. In this question, select the choice that is MOST relevant to the conclusion.
    I. On the planet of Zeinon there are only two different eye colors and only two different hair colors.
    II. Half of those beings with purple hair have golden eyes.
    III. There are more inhabitants with purple hair than there are inhabitants with silver hair.
    IV. One-third of those with silver hair have green eyes.
    CONCLUSION: There are more golden-eyed beings on Zeinon than green-eyed ones.
    A. The conclusion is proved by sentences I-IV.
    B. The conclusion is disproved by sentences I-IV.
    C. The facts are not sufficient to prove or disprove the conclusion.

33. In this question, select the choice that is MOST relevant to the conclusion.
    John and Kevin are leaving Amaranth to go to school in Bethany. They've decided to rent a small truck to move their possessions. Joe's Truck Rental charges $100 plus 30¢ a mile. National Movers charges $50 more but gives free mileage for the first 100 miles. After the first 100 miles, they charge 25¢ a mile.
    CONCLUSION: John and Kevin rent their truck from National Movers because it is cheaper.
    A. The conclusion is proved by the facts in the above paragraph.
    B. The conclusion is disproved by the facts in the above paragraph.
    C. The facts are not sufficient to prove or disprove the conclusion.

34. For this question, select the choice that supports the information given in the passage.

    Municipalities in Country X are divided into villages, towns, and cities. A village has a population of 5,000 or less. The population of a town ranges from 5,001 to 15,000. In order to be incorporated as a city, the municipality must have a population over 15,000. If, after a village becomes a town, or a town becomes a city, the population drops below the minimum required (for example, the population of a city goes below 15,000), and stays below the minimum for more than ten years, it loses its current status, and drops to the next category. As soon as a municipality rises in population to the next category (village to town, for example), however, it is immediately reclassified to the next category.

    In the 2000 census, Plainfield had a population of 12,000. Between 2000 and 2010, Plainfield grew 10%, and between 2010 and 2020 Plainfield grew another 20%. The population of Springdale doubled from 2000 to 2010, and increased 25% from 2010 to 2020. The city of Smallville's population, 20,283, has not changed significantly in recent years. Granton had a population of 25,000 people in 1990, and has decreased 25% in each ten year period since then. Ellenville had a population of 4,283 in 1990, and grew 5% in each ten year period since 1990.

In 2020,
- A. Plainfield, Smallville, and Granton are cities.
- B. Smallville is a city, Granton is a town, and Ellenville is a village.
- C. Springdale, Granton, and Ellenville are towns.
- D. Plainfield and Smallville are cities, and Ellenville is a town.

35. For this question, select the choice that is MOST relevant to the conclusion.

    A study was done for a major food-distributing firm to determine if there is any difference in the kind of caffeine containing products used by people of different ages. A sample of one thousand people between the ages of twenty and fifty were drawn from selected areas in the country. They were divided equally into three groups.

    Those individuals who were 20-29 were designated Group A, those 30-39 were Group B, and those 40-50 were placed in Group C.

    It was found that on the average, Group A drank 1.8 cups of coffee, Group B 3.1, and Group C 2.5 cups of coffee daily. Group A drank 2.1 cups of tea, Group B drank 1.2, and Group C drank 2.6 cups of tea daily. Group A drank 3 1.8 ounces glasses of cola, Group B drank 1.9, and Group C drank 1.5 glasses of cola daily.

    CONCLUSION: According to the study, the average person in the 20-29 age group drinks less tea daily than the average person in the 40-50 age group, but drinks more coffee daily than the average person in the 30-39 age group drinks cola.
    - A. The conclusion is proved by the facts in the above paragraph.
    - B. The conclusion is disproved by the facts in the above paragraph.
    - C. The facts are not sufficient to prove or disprove the conclusion.

36. For this question, select the choice that is MOST relevant to the conclusion
    - I. Mary is taller than Jane but shorter than Dale.
    - II. Fred is taller than Mary but shorter than Steven.
    - III. Dale is shorter than Steven but taller than Elizabeth.
    - IV. Elizabeth is taller than Mary but not as tall as Fred.

    CONCLUSION: Dale is taller than Fred.
    - A. The conclusion is proved by sentences I-IV.
    - B. The conclusion is disproved by sentences I-IV.
    - C. The facts are not sufficient to prove or disprove the conclusion.

37. For this question, select the choice that is MOST relevant to the conclusion.
    - I. Main Street is between Spring Street and Glenn Blvd.
    - II. Hawley Avenue is one block south of Spring Street and three blocks north of Main Street.
    - III. Glenn Street is five blocks south of Elm and four blocks south of Main.
    - IV. All the streets mentioned are parallel to one another.

    CONCLUSION: Elm Street is between Hawley Avenue and Glenn Blvd.
    - A. The conclusion is proved by the facts in sentences I-IV.
    - B. The conclusion is disproved by the facts in sentences I-IV.
    - C. The facts are not sufficient to prove or disprove the conclusion.

38. For this question, select the choice that is MOST relevant to the conclusion. 38.____
   I. Train A leaves the town of Hampshire every day at 5:50 A.M. and arrives in New London at 6:42 A.M.
   II. Train A leaves New London at 7:00 A.M. and arrives in Kellogsville at 8:42 A.M.
   III. Train B leaves Kellogsville at 8:00 A.M. and arrives in Hampshire at 10:45 A.M.
   IV. Due to the need for repairs, there is just one railroad track between New London and Hampshire.
   CONCLUSION: It is impossible for Train A and Train B to follow these schedules without colliding.
   A. The conclusion is proved by the facts in sentences I-IV.
   B. The conclusion is disproved by the facts in sentences I-IV.
   C. The facts are not sufficient to prove or disprove the conclusion.

KEY (CORRECT ANSWERS)

1.	D	11.	C	21.	D	31.	C
2.	B	12.	C	22.	A	32.	A
3.	E	13.	D	23.	C	33.	C
4.	B	14.	B	24.	B	34.	B
5.	C	15.	E	25.	E	35.	B
6.	A	16.	B	26.	C	36.	C
7.	D	17.	A	27.	B	37.	A
8.	B	18.	B	28.	E	38.	B
9.	B	19.	D	29.	B		
10.	B	20.	E	30.	D		

SOLUTIONS TO QUESTIONS

1. The answer is D. This statement weakens the conclusion, but does not disprove it. If a new branch of the community college opened in September, it could possibly bring in new business for Mr. Bryant. Since it states in the conclusion that Mr. Bryant felt there would not be enough new business to support the additional stores, this would tend to disprove the conclusion. Choice C would not be correct because it's possible that he felt that the students would not have enough additional money to support his new venture, or would not be interested in his clothing styles. It's also possible that the majority of the students already live in the area, so that they wouldn't really be a new customer population. This type of question is tricky, and can initially be very confusing, so don't feel badly if you missed it. Most people need to practice with a few of these types of questions before they feel comfortable recognizing exactly what they're being asked to do.

2. The answer is B. It supports the conclusion because the closing of the factory would probably take money and customers out of the town, causing Mr. Bryant to lose some of his present business. It doesn't prove the conclusion, however, because we don't know how large the factory was. It's possible that only a small percentage of the population was employed there, or that they found other jobs.

3. The answer is E. The fact that the number of children per household dropped slightly nationwide in the decade is irrelevant. Statistics showing a drop nationwide doesn't mean that there was a drop in the number of children per household in Mr. Bryant's hometown. This is a tricky question, as choice B, supporting the conclusion but not proving it, may seem reasonable. If the number of children per household declined nationwide, then it may not seem unreasonable to feel that this would support Mr. Bryant's decision not to expand his business. However, we're preparing you for promotional exams, not "real life." One of the difficult things about taking exams is that sometimes you're forced to make a choice between two statements that both seem like they could be the possible answer. What you need to do in that case is choose the best choice. Becoming annoyed or frustrated with the question won't really help much. If there's a review of the exam, you can certainly appeal the question. There have been many cases where, after an appeal, two possible choices have been allowed as correct answers. We've included this question, however, to help you see what to do should you get a question like this. It's most important not to get rattled, and to select the BEST choice. In this case, the connection between the statistical information and Mr. Bryant's decision is pretty remote. If the question had said that the number of children in Mr. Bryant's <u>town</u> had decreased, then choice B would have been a more reasonable choice. It could also help in this situation to visualize the situation. Picture Mr. Bryant in his armchair reading that, nationwide, the average number of children per household has declined slightly. How likely would this be to influence his decision, especially since he sells men's and women's clothing? It would take a while for this decline in population to show up, and we're not even sure if it applies to Mr. Bryant's hometown. Don't feel badly if you missed this; it was tricky. The more of these you do, the more comfortable you'll feel.

4. The answer is B. If a new clothing boutique specializing in casual women's clothing were to open soon, this would lend support to Mr. Bryant's decision not to expand, but would not prove that he had actually made the decision to expand. A new women's clothing boutique would most likely be in competition with his existing business, thus making any possible expansion a riskier venture. We can't be sure from this, however, that he didn't go ahead and expand his business despite the increased competition. Choice A, proves the conclusion, would only be the answer if we could be absolutely sure from the statement that Mr. Bryant had actually <u>not</u> expanded his business.

5. The answer is C. This statement disproves the conclusion. In order for his sister to buy several items for her baby at Mr. Bryant's store, he would have to have changed his business to include children's clothing.

6. The answer is A. It definitely proves the conclusion. The passage states that Mr. Bryan's store had been in business since 1920. A pie baked in honor of his store's 100th anniversary would have to be presented sometime in 2020. The conclusion states that he made his decision not to expand on November 7, 2018. If, more than a year later Mrs. MacIntyre comments that his store has maintained the same look and feel over the years, it could not have been expanded, or otherwise significantly changed.

7. The answer is D. If Mr. Bryant's aunt lent him $50,000 in October, this would tend to weaken the conclusion, which took place in November. Because it was stated that Mr. Bryant would need to borrow money in order to expand his business, it would be logical to assume that if he borrowed money he had decided to expand his business, weakening the conclusion. The reason C, disproves the conclusion, is not the correct answer is because we can't be sure Mr. Bryant didn't borrow the money for another reason.

8. The answer is B. If Mr. Bryant's town is eligible for federal funds to encourage the location of new businesses in the central district, this would tend to support his decision not to expand his business. Funds to encourage new business would increase the likelihood of there being additional competition for Mr. Bryant's store to contend with. Since we can't say for sure that there would be direct competition from a new business, however, choice A would be incorrect. Note that this is also a tricky question. You might have thought that the new funds weakened the conclusion because it would mean that Mr. Bryant could easily get the money he needed. Mr. Bryant is expanding his present business, not creating a <u>new</u> business. Therefore, he is not eligible for the funding.

9. The answer is B. This is a very tricky question. It's stated that 59% of car occupants don't use seat belts. The legislature is considering the use of air bags because of safety issues. The advantage of air bags over seat belts is that they inflate upon impact, and don't require car occupants to do anything with them ahead of time. Since the population has strongly resisted using seat belts, the air bags could become even more important in saving lives. Since saving lives is the purpose of the proposed legislation, the information that a small percentage of people use seat belts could be helpful to the passage of the legislation. We can't be sure that this is reason enough for the legislature to vote for the legislation, however, so choice A in incorrect.

10. The answer is B, as the information that 5,900 lives could be saved would tend to support the conclusion. Saving that many lives through the use of air bags could be a very persuasive reason to vote for the legislation. Since we don't know for sure that it's enough of a compelling reason for the legislature to vote for the legislation, however, choice A could not be the answer.

11. The answer is C, disproves the conclusion. If the legislation had been passed as stated in the conclusion, there would be no reason to appoint someone head of an advisory committee six days later to analyze the "feasibility of the proposed legislation." The key word here is "proposed." If it has been proposed, it means it hasn't been passed. This contradicts the conclusion and, therefore, disproves it.

12. The answer is C, disproves the conclusion. If the legislation had passed, there would be no reason for supporters of the legislation to accuse the legislature of rejecting the legislation for political reasons. This question may have seemed so obvious that you might have thought there was a trick to it. Exams usually have a few obvious questions, which will trip you up if you begin reading too much into them.

13. The answer is D, as this would tend to disprove the conclusion. A projected dramatic rise in imported cars could be very harmful to the country's economy and could be a very good reason for some legislators to vote against the proposed legislation. It would be assuming too much to choose C, however, because we don't know if they actually did vote against it.

14. The answer is B. This information would tend to support the passage of the legislation. The estimate of the cost of the air bags is $800 less than the cost estimated by opponents, and it's stated that the protection would be more reliable than any other type of seat belt. Both of these would be good arguments in favor of passing the legislation. Since we don't know for sure, however, how persuasive they actually were, choice A would not be the correct choice.

15. The answer is E, as this is irrelevant information. It really doesn't matter whether auto sales in 2001 have increased slightly over the previous year. If the air bag legislation were to go into effect in 2004, that might make the information somehow more relevant. But the air bag legislation would not take effect until 2009, so the information is irrelevant, since it tells us nothing about the state of the auto industry then.

16. The answer is B, supports the conclusion. This is a tricky question. While at first it might seem to prove the conclusion, we can't be sure that the air bag legislation is responsible for the drop in automobile deaths. It's possible air bags came into popular use without the legislation, or with different legislation. There's no way we can be sure that it was the proposed legislation mandating the use of air bags that was responsible.

17. The answer is A. If, in June of 2009, the lobbyist received a bonus "for her work on the air bag legislation," we can be sure that the legislation passed. This proves the conclusion.

18. The answer is B. This is another tricky question. A three-fold stock increase would strongly suggest that the legislation had been passed, but it's possible that factors other than the air bag legislation caused the increase. Note that the stock is in "crash protection

equipment." Nowhere in the statement does it say air bags. Seat belts, motorcycle helmets, and collapsible bumpers are all crash protection equipment and could have contributed to the increase. This is just another reminder to read carefully because the questions are often designed to mislead you.

19. The answer is D. This would tend to weaken the conclusion because Joan is very fond of her mother and she would not want to upset her unnecessarily. It does not prove it, however, because if Joan strongly feels she is right, she probably wouldn't let her mother's opinion sway her. Choice E would also not be correct, because we cannot assume that Joan's mother's opinion is of so little importance to her as to be considered irrelevant.

20. The answer is E. The statement is irrelevant. We are told that Joan's income has doubled but we are not old why. The phrase "six months after the interview" can be misleading in that it leads us to assume that the increase and the interview are related. Her income could have doubled because she regained her popularity but it could also have come from stocks or some other business venture. Because we are not given any reason for her income doubling, it would be impossible to say whether or not this statement proves or disproves the conclusion. Choice E is the best choice of the five possible choices. One of the problems with promotional exams is that sometimes you need to select a choice you're not crazy about. In this case, "not having enough information to made a determination" would be the best choice. However, that's not an option, so you're forced to work with what you've got. On these exams it's sometimes like voting for President; you have to pick the "lesser of the two evils" or the least awful choice. In this case, the information is more irrelevant to the conclusion than it is anything else.

21. The answer is D, weakens the conclusion. We've been told that Joan's agent feels that she should apologize. If he is pleased with her interview, then it would tend to weaken the conclusion but not disprove it. We can't be sure that he hasn't had a change of heart, or that there weren't other parts of the interview he liked so much that they outweighed her unwillingness to apologize.

22. The answer is A. The conclusion states that Joan will donate $1 to the Cellulite Prevention League for every pound the actress loses. Joan's sister's financial report on the League's activities directly supports and proves the conclusion.

23. The answer is C, disproves the conclusion. If the magazine receives many letters commending Joan for her courage in apologizing, this directly contradicts the conclusion, which states that Joan didn't apologize.

24. The answer is B. It was stated in the passage that two of Joan's performances were cancelled after the controversy first occurred. The cancellation of another performance immediately after her interview was published would tend to support the conclusion that she refused to apologize. Because we can't be sure, however, that her performance wasn't cancelled for another reason, choice A would be incorrect.

25. The answer is E, as this information is irrelevant. Postponing the article an extra week does not affect Joan's decision or the public's reaction to it.

13 (#1)

26. The answer is C. If 500 new employees are hired to handle the "increased paperwork created by the new tax on DVDs," this would directly contradict the conclusion, which states that the legislature defeated both bills. (They should all be this easy.)

27. The answer is B. The results of the study would support the conclusion. If implementing the legislation was going to be so costly, it is likely that the legislature would vote against it. Choice A is not the answer, however, because we can't be sure that the legislature didn't pass it anyway.

28. The answer is E. It's irrelevant to the conclusion that 80% of all those working in the entertainment industry own DVD recorders. Sometimes if you're not sure about these, it can help a lot to try and visualize the situation. Why would someone voting on this legislation care about this fact? It doesn't seem to be the kind of information that would make any difference or impact upon the conclusion.

29. The answer is B. The head of the law enforcement agency's statement that the legislation would be unenforceable would support the conclusion. It's possible that many legislators would question why they should bother to pass legislation that would be impossible to enforce. Choice A would be incorrect, however, because we can't be sure that the legislation wasn't passed in spite of his statement.

30. The answer is D. This would tend to weaken the conclusion because the prospect of several large companies going bankrupt would seem to be a good argument in favor of the legislation. The possible loss of jobs and businesses would be a good reason for some people to vote for the legislation. We can't be sure, however, that this would be a competing enough reason to ensure passage of the legislation so choice C is incorrect.

This concludes our section on the "Validity of Conclusion" type of questions. We hope these weren't too horrible for you. It's important to keep in mind <u>exactly</u> what you've been given and <u>exactly</u> what they want you to do with it. It's also necessary to remember that you may have to choose between two possible answers. In that case, you must choose the one that seems the best. Sometimes you may think there is no good answer. You will probably be right, but you can't let that upset you. Just choose the one you dislike the least.

We want to repeat that it is unlikely that this exact format will appear on the exam. The skills required to answer these questions, however, are the same as those you'll need for the exam so we suggest that you review this section before taking the actual exam.

31. The answer is C. This next set of questions requires you to "switch gears" slightly, and get used to different formats. In this type of question, you have to decide whether the conclusion is proved by the facts give, disproved by the facts given, or neither because note enough information has been provided. Fortunately, unlike the previous questions, you don't have to decide whether particular facts support or don't support the conclusion. This type of question is more straight forward, but the reasoning behind it is the same. We are told that the Bills have won two games less than the Patriots, and that the Patriots are in first place and the Bills are in second place. We are also told that there are two games left to play, and that they won't play each other again. The conclusion states that the Bills won the division. Is there anything in the four statements that would prove this? We have

no idea what the outcome of the last two games of the season was. The Bills and Patriots could have ended up tied at the end of the season, or the Bills could have lost both or one of their last games while the Patriots did the same. There might even be another team tied for first or second place with the Bills or Patriots. Since we don't know for sure, Choice A is incorrect. Choice B is trickier. It might seem at first glance that the best the Bills could do would be to tie the Patriots if the Patriots lost their last two games and the Bills won their last two games. But it would be too much to assume that there is no procedure for a tiebreaker that wouldn't give the Bills the division championship. Since we don't know what the rules are in the event of a tie (for example, what if a tie was decided on the results of what happened when the two teams had played each other, or on the best record in the division, or on most points scored?), we can't say for sure that it would be impossible for the Bills to win their division. For this reason, choice C is the answer, as we don't have enough information to prove or disprove the conclusion. This question looked more difficult than it actually was. It's important to disregard any factors outside of the actual question, and to focus only on what you've been given. In this case, as on all of these types of questions, what you know or don't know about a subject is actually irrelevant. It's best to concentrate only on the actual facts given.

32. The answer is A. The conclusion is proved by the facts given.

    In this type of problem, it is usually best to pull as many facts as possible from the sentences and then put them into a simpler form. The phrasing and the order of exam questions are designed to be confusing so you need to restate things as clearly as possible by eliminating the extras.

    Sentence I tells us that there are only two possible colors for eyes and two for hair. Looking at the other sentences we learn that eyes are either green or gold and that hair is either silver or purple. If half the beings with purple hair have golden eyes, then the other half must have green eyes since it is the only other eye color. Likewise, if one-third of those with silver hair have green eyes, the other two-thirds must have golden eyes.

    This information makes it clear that there are more golden-eyed beings on Zeinon than green-eyed ones. It doesn't matter that we don't know exactly how many are actually living on the planet. The number of those with gold eyes (1/2 plus 2/3) will always be greater than the number of those with green eyes (1/2 plus 1/3), no matter what the actual figures might be. Sentence III is totally irrelevant because even if there were more silver-haired inhabitants it would not affect the conclusion.

33. The answer is C. The conclusion is neither proved nor disproved by the facts because we don't know how many miles Bethany is from Amoranth.

    With this type of question, if you're not sure how to approach it, you can always substitute in a range of "real numbers" to see what the result would be. If they were 200 miles apart, Joe's Truck Rental would be cheaper because they would charge a total of $160 while National Movers would charge $175.

    Joe's - $100 plus .30 x 200 (or $60) = $160
    National - $150 plus .25 x 100 (or $25) = $175

    If the towns were 600 miles apart, however, National Movers would be cheaper. The cost of renting from National would be $275 compared to the $280 charged by Joe's Trucking.

    Joe's - $100 plus .30 x 600 (or $180) = $280
    National - $150 plus .25 x 500 (or $125) = $275

15 (#1)

34. The answer is B. We've varied the format once more, but the reasoning is similar. This is a tedious question that is more like a math question, but we wanted to give you some practice with this type, just in case. You won't be able to do this question if you've forgotten how to do percents. Many exams require this knowledge, so if you feel you need a review we suggest you read Booklets 1, 2 or 3 in this series.

The only way to attack this problem is to go through each choice until you find the one that is correct. Choice A states that Plainfield, Smallville, and Granton are cities. Let's begin with Plainfield. The passage states that in 1990 Plainfield had a population of 12,000, and that it grew 10% between 1990 and 2000, and another 20% between 2000 and 2010. Ten percent of 12,000 is 1200 (12,000 x .10 = 1200). Therefore, the population grew from 12,000 in 1990 to 12,000 + 1200 between 1990 and 2000. At the time of the 2000 Census, Plainfield's population was 13,200. It then grew another 20% between 2000 and 2010, so, 13,200 x .20 = 2640. 13,200 plus the additional increase of 2640 would make the population of Plainfield 15,840. This would qualify it as a city, since its population is over 15,000. Since a change upward in the population of a municipality is re-classified immediately, Plainfield would have become a city right away. So far, statement A is true. The passage states that Smallville's population has not changed significantly in the last twenty years. Since Smallville's population was 20,283, Smallville would still be a city. Granton had a population of 25,000 (what a coincidence that so any of these places have such nice, even numbers) in 1980. The population has decreased 25% in each ten year period since that time. So from 1980 to 1990, the population decreased 25%. 25,000 x .25 = 6,250. 25,000 minus 6,250 = 18,750. So the population of Granton in 1990 would have been 18,750. (Or, you could have saved a step and multiplied 25,000 by .75 to get 18,750.) The population from 1990 to 2000 decreased an additional 25%. So: 18,750 x .25 = 4,687.50. 18,750 minus 4,687.50 = 14,062.50. Or: 18,750 x .75 = 14,062.50. (Don't let the fact that a half of a person is involved confuse you; these are exam questions, not real life.) From 2000 to 2010 the population decreased an additional 25%. This would mean that Granton's population was below 15,000 for more than ten years, so it's status as a city would have changed to that of a town, which would make choice A incorrect.

Choice B states that Smallville is a city and Granton is a town, which we know to be true from the information above. Choice B is correct so far. We next need to determine if Ellenville is a village. Ellenville had a population of 4,283 in 1980, and increased 5% in each ten year period since 1980. 4,283 x .05 = 214.15. 4,283 plus 214.15 = 4,497.15, so Ellenville's population from 1980 to 1990 increased to 4,497.15. (Or: 4,283 x 1.05 – 4,497.15.) From 1990 to 2000 Ellenville's population increased another 5%: 4,497.15 x .05 = 224.86. 4,497.15 plus 224.86 = 4,772.01 (or: 4,497.15 x 1.05 = 4,722.01.) From 2000 to 2010, Ellenville's population increased another 5%: 4,722.01 x .05 = 236.10. 4,722.01 plus 236.10 = 4,958.11. (Or: 4,722.01 x 1.05 = 4,958.11.).

Ellenville's population is still under 5,000 in 2010, so it would continue to be classified as a village. Since all three statements in choice B are true, choice B must be the answer. However, we'll go through the other choices. Choice C states that Springdale is a town. The passage tells us that the population of Springdale doubled from 1990 to 2000, and increased 25% from 2000 to 2010. It doesn't give us any actual population figures, however, so it's impossible to know what the population of Springdale is, making choice C incorrect. Choice C also states that Granton is a town, which is true, and that Ellenville is a town, which is false (from choice B we know it's a village). Choice D states that Plainfield and Smallville are cities, which is information we already know is true, and that Ellenville is a town. Since Ellenville is a village, choice D is also incorrect.

This was a lot of work for just one question and we doubt you'll get one like this on this section of the exam, but we included it just in case. On an exam, you can always put a check mark next to a question like this and come back to it later, if you feel you're pressed for time and cold spend your time more productively on other, less time-consuming problems.

35. The answer is B. This question requires very careful reading. It's best to break the conclusion down into smaller parts in order to solve the problem. The first half of the conclusion states that the average person in the 20-29 age group (Group A) drinks less tea daily than the average person in the 40-50 age group (Group C). The average person in Group A drinks 2.1 cups of tea daily, while the average person in Group C drinks 2.6 cups of tea daily. Since 2.1 is less than 2.6, the conclusion is correct so far. The second half of the conclusion states that the average person in Group A drinks more coffee daily than the average person in the 30-39 age group (Group B) drinks cola. The average person in Group A drinks 1.8 cups of coffee daily, while the average person in Group B drinks 1.9 glasses of cola. This disproves the conclusion, which states that the average person in Group A drinks more coffee daily than the average person in Group B drinks cola.

36. The answer is C. The easiest way to approach a problem that deals with the relationship between a number of different people or things is to set up a diagram. This type of problem is usually too confusing to do in your head. For this particular problem, the "diagram" could be a line, one end of which would be labeled tall and the other end labeled short. Then, taking one sentence at a time, place the people on the line to see where they fall in relation to one another.

The diagram of the first sentence would look like this:

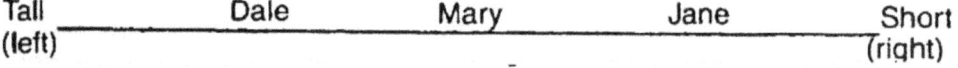

Mary is taller than Jane but shorter than Dale, so she would fall somewhere between the two of them. We have placed tall on the left and labeled it left just to make the explanation easier. You could just as easily have reversed the position.

The second sentence places Fred somewhere to the left of Mary because he is taller than she is. Steven would be to the left of Fred for the same reason. At this point we don't know whether Steven and Fred are taller or shorter than Dale. The new diagram would look like this:

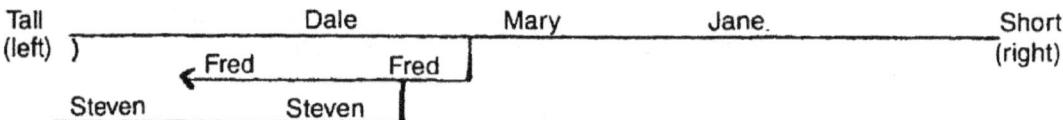

The third sentence introduces Elizabeth, presenting a new problem. Elizabeth can be anywhere to the right of Dale. Don't make the mistake of assuming she falls between Dale and Mary. At this point we don't know where she fits in relation to Mary, Jane, or even Fred.

We do get information about Steven, however. He is taller than Dale so he would be to the left of Dale. Since he is also taller than Fred (see sentence II), we know that Steven is the tallest person thus far. The diagram would now look like this:

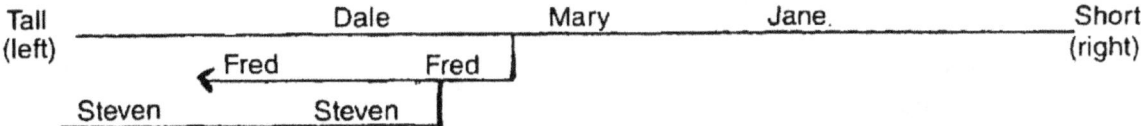

Fred's height is somewhere between Steven and Mary, Elizabeth's anywhere between Dale and the end of the line.

The fourth sentence tells us where Elizabeth stands, in relation to Fred and the others in the problem. The fact that she is taller than Mary means she is also taller than Jane. The final diagram would look like this:

| Tall (left) | Steven | Dale | Elizabeth | Mary | Jane | Short (right) |

with Fred bracketed between Steven and Dale area.

We still don't know whether Dale or Fred is taller, however. Therefore, the conclusion that Dale is taller than Fred can't be proved. It also can't be disproved because we don't know for sure that he isn't. The answer has to be choice C, as the conclusion can't be proved or disproved.

37. The answer is A. This is another problem that is easiest for most people if they make a diagram. Sentence I states that Main Street is between Spring Street and Glenn Blvd. At this point we don't know if they are next to each other or if they are separated by a number of streets. Therefore, you should leave space between streets as you plot your first diagram.

The order of the streets could go either:

    Spring St.   or   Glenn Blvd.
    Main St.   Main St.
    Glenn Blvd.   Spring St.

Sentence II states that Hawley Street is one block south of Spring Street and 3 blocks north of Main Street. Because most people think in terms of north as above and south as below and because it was stated that Hawley is one block south of Spring Street and three blocks north of Main Street, the next diagram could look like this:

18 (#1)

<u>Spring</u>
<u>Hawley</u>

――――

<u>Main</u>
<u>Glenn</u>

The third sentence states that Glenn Street is five blocks south of Elm and four blocks south of Main. It could look like this:

<u>Spring</u>
<u>Hawley</u>

――――

<u>Elm</u>
<u>Main</u>

――――
――――

<u>Glenn</u>

The conclusion states that Elm Street is between Hawley Avenue and Glenn Blvd. From the above diagram, we can see that this is the case.

38. The answer is B. For most people, the best way to do this problem is to draw a diagram, plotting the course of both trains. Sentence I states that Train A leaves Hampshire at 5:50 A.M. and reaches New London at 6:42. Your first diagram might look like this:

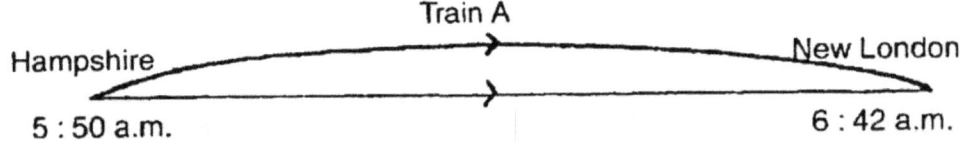

Sentence II states that the train leaves New London at 7:00 a.m. and arrives in Kellogsville at 8:42 a.m. The diagram might now look like this:

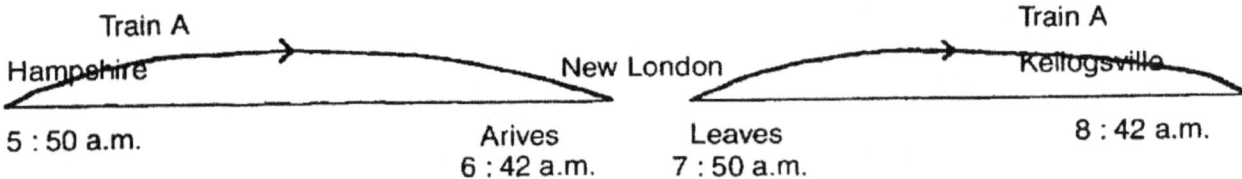

Sentence III gives us the rest of the information that must be included in the diagram. It introduces Train B, which moves in the opposite direction, leaving Kellogsville at 8:00 a.m. and arriving at Hampshire at 10:42 a.m. The final diagram might look like this:

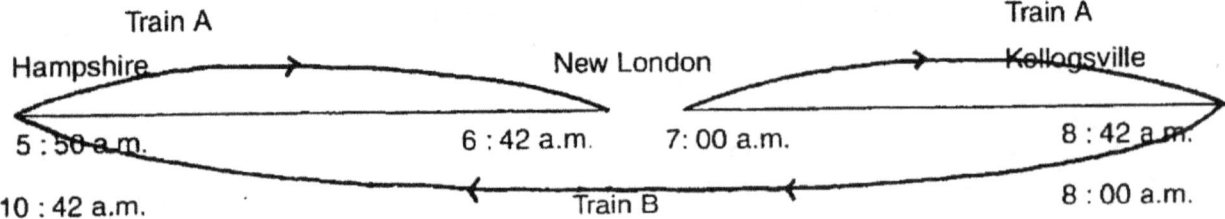

19 (#1)

As you can see from the diagram, the routes of the two trains will overlap somewhere between Kellogsville and New London. If you read sentence IV quickly and assumed that that was the section with only one track, you probably would have assumed that there would have had to be a collision. Sentence IV states, however, that there is only one railroad track between New London and Hampshire. That is the only section, then, where the two trains could collide. By the time Train B gets to that section, however, Train A will have passed it. The two trains will pass each other somewhere between New London and Kellogsville, not New London and Hampshire.

EXAMINATION SECTION
TEST 1

DIRECTIONS: Below are 10 groups of statements and conclusions, numbered 1 through 10. For each group of statements, select the one conclusion lettered A, B, C, which is fully supported by and is based SOLELY on the statements. PRINT THE LETTER OF THE CORRECT ANSWER IN THE SPACE AT THE RIGHT.

1. He is either approved or disapproved for this examination. But, he is not approved. Therefore, he is

    A. qualified
    B. disapproved
    C. a taxpayer

    1.____

2. In planning the itinerary for Mr. Kane, his secretary told him: Route 20 runs parallel to Route 6. Route 6 runs parallel to Route 18.
   Mr. Kane concluded that,
   Therefore, Route

    A. 20 is north of Route 6
    B. 18 intersects Route 20
    C. 20 is parallel to Route 18

    2.____

3. Either the valedictorian is more intelligent than the salutatorian, or as intelligent, or less intelligent.
   But the valedictorian is not more intelligent, nor is she less intelligent.
   Therefore, the valedictorian is

    A. less intelligent than the salutatorian
    B. as intelligent as the salutatorian
    C. more intelligent than the salutatorian

    3.____

4. If the date for the examination is changed, it will be held July 28, or it will be postponed until October 15.
   The date is not changed.
   Therefore, the examination

    A. will probably be held July 28
    B. date is uncertain
    C. will be held July 28, or it will be postponed until October 15

    4.____

5. Joan transcribes faster than Nancy.
   Nancy transcribes faster than Anne.
   Therefore,

    A. Nancy transcribes faster than Joan
    B. Joan transcribes faster than Anne
    C. Nancy has had longer experience than Anne in taking dictation

    5.____

6. The files in Division D contain either pending matter, completed case records, or dead material.
   They do not contain pending matter.
   Therefore, they contain

    6.____

81

A. completed case records
B. completed case records and dead material
C. either completed case records or dead material

7. Either stenographer B in pool C types faster than stenographer A in pool D, or she types at the same rate as stenographer A, or she types slower than stenographer A. But, she does not type faster than stenographer A, nor does she type slower than stenographer Therefore, stenographer

   A. B does not type as fast as stenographer A
   B. B is more efficient than stenographer A
   C. A types as fast as stenographer B

8. Miss Andre can be eligible for retirement when she has been in city service 35 years, or if she is 55 years of age. She is fifty-four years old and has been in city service 36 years. Therefore, she

   A. is not eligible for retirement now
   B. is eligible for retirement now
   C. will be eligible for retirement only if she stays in city service for another year

9. If K is L, O is P; if M is N, Q is R.
   Either K is L, or M is N.
   Therefore,

   A. K is P or M is R
   B. either O is P or Q is R
   C. the conclusion is uncertain

10. If the employee is in error, the supervisor's refusal to listen to his side is unreasonable. If he is not in error, the supervisor's refusal is unjust. But the employee is in error or he is not.
    Therefore, the supervisor's refusal

    A. may be considered later
    B. is either unreasonable or it is unjust
    C. is justifiable

KEY (CORRECT ANSWERS)

1. B	6. C
2. C	7. C
3. B	8. B
4. B	9. B
5. B	10. B

TEST 2

Questions 1-5

DIRECTIONS: Below are 5 groups of statements and conclusions, numbered 1 through 5. For each group of statements, select the one conclusion lettered A, B, C, which is fully supported by and is based SOLELY on the statements. *PRINT THE LETTER OF THE CORRECT ANSWER IN THE SPACE AT THE RIGHT.*

1. Three desks are placed in a straight row just inside the door in our office. Desk 1 is farther from the door than Desk 2. Desk 3 is farther from the door than Desk 1. Which desk is in the middle position from the door? Desk

    A. 1   B. 2   C. 3

    1.____

2. The problem is either correct or incorrect or is unsolvable. The problem is not correct. Therefore, the

    A. problem is incorrect
    B. problem is either incorrect or is unsolvable
    C. conclusion is uncertain

    2.____

3. Village E is situated between City F and Village G. City F is situated between Village G and Town H. Therefore, Village E is

    A. not situated between Village G and Town H
    B. situated between City F and Town H
    C. situated nearer to City F than to Town H

    3.____

4. Jurisdiction No. 1 is between Jurisdictions No. 2 and No. 3. Jurisdiction No. 2 is between Jurisdictions No. 3 and No. 4. Therefore, Jurisdiction No. 1 is

    A. not between Jurisdictions No. 3 and No. 4
    B. between Jurisdictions No. 2 and No. 4
    C. nearer to Jurisdiction No. 2 than to No. 4

    4.____

5. Five candidates (A, B, C, D, and E) are seated in the same room. D is between A and B, E is between A and D; C is the same distance from A and E, and D is the same distance from A and B. Therefore,

    A. E is nearer to B than to A
    B. C is nearer to E than to D
    C. B is nearer to E than to D

    5.____

Questions 6-10.

DIRECTIONS: Each question or incomplete statement is followed by several suggested answers or completions. Select the one that BEST answers the question or completes the statement. *PRINT THE LETTER OF THE CORRECT ANSWER IN THE SPACE AT THE RIGHT.*

6. If John is older than Mary and Mary is younger than Jane, then

    A. twice Mary's age is less than the sum of the ages of John and Jane
    B. the sum of the ages of John and Mary exceeds the age of Jane
    C. the ages of John and Jane are equal
    D. three times Mary's age equals the sum of the ages of John and Jane

7. John is older than Mary, Henry is older than Mary.
   It follows, therefore, that

    A. John and Henry are the same age
    B. the sum of the ages of John and Mary exceeds the age of Henry
    C. Mary's age is less than half of the sum of John's and Henry's ages
    D. none of the preceding three statements is true

8. The average of 9 numbers is 70.
   It follows that

    A. the sum of the numbers is 630
    B. the median of the numbers is 70
    C. the median of the numbers cannot be 70
    D. no two of the numbers can be equal

9. John is twice as old as Mary.
   The only statement about their ages which is NOT true is

    A. in five years, John will be twice as old as Mary
    B. in five years, the sum of their ages will be 10 more than the present sum of their ages
    C. Mary's present age is one-third of the sum of their present ages
    D. two years ago, the difference between their ages was the same as it will be two years hence

10. A is taller than B; C is 2 inches shorter than B.
    The one statement of the following four statements which is NOT necessarily true is

    A. B is taller than C
    B. A is taller than C
    C. A is taller than C by more than 2 inches
    D. B's height is the average of the heights of A and C

KEY (CORRECT ANSWERS)

1.	A	6.	A
2.	B	7.	C
3.	C	8.	D
4.	C	9.	A
5.	B	10.	D

TEST 3

DIRECTIONS: Each question or incomplete statement is followed by several suggested answers or completions. Select the one that BEST answers the question or completes the statement. *PRINT THE LETTER OF THE CORRECT ANSWER IN THE SPACE AT THE RIGHT.*

1. A stenographer can BEST deal with the situation which arises when her pencil breaks during dictation by

    A. asking the person dictating to lend her one
    B. being equipped at every dictation with several pencils
    C. going back to her desk to secure another one
    D. making a call to the supply room for some pencils

    1._____

2. Accuracy is of greater importance than speed in filing CHIEFLY because

    A. city offices have a tremendous amount of filing to do
    B. fast workers are usually inferior workers
    C. there is considerable difficulty in locating materials which have been filed incorrectly
    D. there are many varieties of filing systems which may be used

    2._____

3. Many persons dictate so rapidly that they pay little attention to matters of punctuation and English, but they expect their stenographers to correct errors.
This statement implies MOST clearly that stenographers should be

    A. able to write acceptable original reports when required
    B. good citizens as well as good stenographers
    C. efficient clerks as well as good stenographers
    D. efficient in language usage

    3._____

4. A typed letter should resemble a picture properly framed.
This statement MOST emphasizes

    A. accuracy   B. speed
    C. convenience   D. neatness

    4._____

5. Of the following, the CHIEF advantage of the use of a mechanical check is that it

    A. guards against tearing in handling the check
    B. decreases the possibility of alteration in the amount of the check
    C. tends to prevent the mislaying and loss of checks
    D. facilitates keeping checks in proper order for mailing

    5._____

6. Of the following, the CHIEF advantage of the use of a dictating machine is that the

    A. stenographer must be able to take rapid dictation
    B. person dictating tends to make few errors
    C. dictator may be dictating letters while the stenographer is busy at some other task
    D. usual noise in an office is lessened

    6._____

7. The CHIEF value of indicating enclosures beneath the identification marks on the lower left side of a letter is that it

   A. acts as a check upon the contents before mailing and upon receiving a letter
   B. helps determine the weight for mailing
   C. is useful in checking the accuracy of typed matter
   D. requires an efficient mailing clerk

8. The one of the following which is NOT an advantage of the window envelope is that it

   A. saves time since the inside address serves also as an outside address
   B. gives protection to the address from wear and tear of the mails
   C. lessens the possibility of mistakes since the address is written only once
   D. tends to be much easier to seal than the plain envelope

9. A question as to proper syllabication of a word at the end of a line may BEST be settled by consulting

   A. the person who dictated the letter
   B. a shorthand manual
   C. a dictionary
   D. a file of letters

10. Mailing a letter which contains many erasures is undesirable CHIEFLY because

    A. paper should not be wasted
    B. some stenographers are able to carry on some of the correspondence in an office without consulting their superiors
    C. correspondence should be neat
    D. erasures indicate that the dictator was not certain of what he intended to say in the letter

KEY (CORRECT ANSWERS)

1. B
2. C
3. D
4. D
5. B
6. C
7. A
8. D
9. C
10. C

TEST 4

DIRECTIONS: Each question or incomplete statement is followed by several suggested answers or completions. Select the one that BEST answers the question or completes the statement. *PRINT THE LETTER OF THE CORRECT ANSWER IN THE SPACE AT THE RIGHT.*

1. A charter operates for a city in somewhat the same fashion as   1.____

    A. the United States Supreme Court functions with regard to federal legislation
    B. the United States Constitution operates for the entire country
    C. the Governor functions for New York State
    D. a lease for a landlord

2. All civil employees should be especially interested in the activities of the United States Supreme Court PRIMARILY because   2.____

    A. its decisions provide certain kinds of important general rules
    B. the Supreme Court consists of nine persons appointed by the President
    C. the American Constitution is the finest document which man has ever produced
    D. the President's plan for reorganization of the court may be revived

3. Of the following, it is most frequently argued that labor problems are of concern to the civil employee PRIMARILY because   3.____

    A. the problems of labor are the same as the problems of government
    B. newspapers carry considerable information about labor problems
    C. the civil employee is a wage or salary earner
    D. a government is of the people, for the people, and by the people

4. Warfare in any part of the world should be of interest to the civil employee PRIMARILY as a result of the fact that   4.____

    A. strict American neutrality is secured by not permitting the sale of munitions to any country at war
    B. war has not been declared though warfare is raging
    C. the United States participates in the meetings of the UN
    D. facilities for transportation and communication have produced a "smaller" world

5. Cities regulate certain aspects of housing CHIEFLY because   5.____

    A. the city is the largest municipality in the country
    B. zoning is the concern of all residents of the city
    C. housing affects health
    D. the state constitution makes regulation optional

6. In general, it is PROBABLY true that the functions which a city administers are those   6.____

    A. most necessary to the preservation of the well-being of its residents
    B. of little or no interest to private business
    C. forbidden to the state
    D. not capable of being financed by private business

7. There is no more convincing mark of a cultured speaker or writer than accuracy of statement.
   This statement stresses the importance of

   A. new ideas
   B. facts
   C. acquiring a pleasing speaking voice
   D. poise

8. When a department is called, the voice which answers the telephone is, to the person calling, the department itself.
   This statement implies *most clearly* that

   A. only one person should answer the telephone in each office
   B. a clerk with a pleasing, courteous telephone manner is an asset to an office
   C. an efficient clerk will terminate all telephone conversations as quickly as possible
   D. making personal telephone calls is looked upon with disfavor in some offices

9. Probably the CHIEF advantage of filling higher vacancies by promotion is that this procedure

   A. stimulates the worker to improve his work and general knowledge and technique
   B. provides an easy check on the work of the individual
   C. eliminates personnel problems in a department
   D. harmonizes the work of one department with that of all other departments

10. Greatest efficiency is reached when filing method and filing clerk are harmoniously adjusted to the needs of an office.
    This statement means *most nearly* that

    A. the filing method is more important than the clerk in securing the successful handling of valuable papers
    B. almost any clerk can do office filing well
    C. a good clerk using a good filing system assures good filing
    D. every office needs a filing system

KEY (CORRECT ANSWERS)

1. B
2. A
3. C
4. D
5. C

6. A
7. B
8. B
9. A
10. C

TEST 5

DIRECTIONS: Each question or incomplete statement is followed by several suggested answers or completions. Select the one that BEST answers the question or completes the statement. *PRINT THE LETTER OF THE CORRECT ANSWER IN THE SPACE AT THE RIGHT.*

1. Your superior, Mr. Hotchkiss, is in conference and has requested that he not be disturbed.
   The condition under which you would MOST probably disturb the conference is:

   A. A Mr. Smith, whom you have not seen before, says he has important business with Mr. Hotchkiss
   B. Mrs. Hotchkiss telephones, saying there has been a serious accident at home
   C. You do not know how a certain letter should be filed and wish to ask the advice of Mr. Hotchkiss
   D. A fellow clerk wishes to ask Mr. Hotchkiss whether a particular city department handles certain matters

2. Your superior directs you to find certain papers. You know the purpose for which the papers are to be used. In the course of your search for the papers, you come across certain material which would be very useful for the purpose to be served by the papers. You should

   A. bring the papers to your superior and ask whether he wants the other materials
   B. go to your superior immediately and ask whether he wishes both the materials and the papers or only one of the two
   C. bring to your superior the other materials, together with the papers you were directed to find
   D. bring only the other materials to your superior and point out the manner in which these materials are of greater value than the papers

3. If a fellow employee asks you a question to which you do not know the answer, you should say,

   A. "I don't know. What's the difference?"
   B. "The answer to that question forms no part of my duties here."
   C. "My dear sir, the thing for you to do is to look the matter up yourself because it is your responsibility, not mine."
   D. "I'm sorry. I don't know."

4. In general, it is PROBABLY true that MOST people are

   A. so self-seeking that they pay no attention to the wants, needs, or behavior of others
   B. so changeable that one never knows what his fellow employee is likely to do next
   C. not worth the trouble to bother about
   D. quite ready to help others

5. Of the following, the one which is NOT a reason for avoiding clerical errors is that

   A. time is lost
   B. money is wasted
   C. many clerks are very intelligent
   D. serious consequences may follow

6. Of the following, the MAIN reason for keeping a careful record of incoming mail is that

   A. some people are less industrious than others
   B. this record helps to speed up outgoing mail
   C. this record is a kind of legal evidence
   D. this information may be useful in answering questions which may arise

7. Of the following, the MAIN reason for using a calculating machine is that

   A. a lesser knowledge of arithmetic is needed
   B. a more attractive product is obtained
   C. greater speed and accuracy are obtained
   D. it is not difficult to learn how to operate a calculating machine

8. Of the following, the MAIN reason for being polite over the telephone is that

   A. persons who are speaking over the telephone cannot see each other
   B. politeness makes for pleasant business relationships
   C. it is not at all difficult or costly to be courteous
   D. one's voice is of great importance because voice reflects mood

9. Because telephone directories contain printed pages, they are called books.
   This statement assumes *most nearly* that

   A. some books do not contain printed pages
   B. not all telephone directories are books which contain printed pages
   C. material which contains printed pages is called a book
   D. all books which contain printed pages are called telephone directories

10. Mr. Cross must be using a budget because he has been able to reduce his unnecessary expenses.
    On the basis of only the material included in this statement, it may MOST accurately be said that this statement assumes that

    A. all people who use budgets lower certain types of expenses
    B. some people who do not use budgets reduce unnecessary expenses
    C. some people who use budgets do not reduce unnecessary expenses
    D. all types of expenses are reduced by the use of a budget

KEY (CORRECT ANSWERS)

1.	B		6.	D
2.	C		7.	C
3.	D		8.	B
4.	D		9.	C
5.	C		10.	A

REASONING AND JUDGMENT

EXAMINATION SECTION
TEST 1

DIRECTIONS: Each question or incomplete statement is followed by several suggested answers or completions. Select the one that BEST answers the question or completes the statement. *PRINT THE LETTER OF THE CORRECT ANSWER IN THE SPACE AT THE RIGHT.*

1. Lapland consists of the most northern parts of Norway, Sweden, and Finland, and the Kola Peninsula in Russia. The inhabitants, called Lapps, are very hardy people who farm and fish for a livelihood. Their meat, milk, and furs come from the reindeer, which is their only domestic animal.
   There is no country named Lapland, so we cannot ask,

   A. "Who is president of Lapland?"
   B. "What kind of education is there in Lapland?"
   C. "What is the climate in Lapland?"
   D. "Are any of the Lapps wealthy?"

   1._____

2. Induction is a method of reasoning by which general laws are inferred from the observation of a large number of individual cases. The laws thus derived are based not upon logical necessity but upon consistency among observations.
   Since any new observation conceivably could fail to follow the inductive law which it would be predicted to follow, an inductive law is never

   A. sought in scientific research
   B. as useful as a deductive law
   C. used as a basis for action
   D. more than probably true

   2._____

3. A lion, finding a hare asleep, was about to devour it when he saw a deer passing. He left the hare and chased the deer, which was so swift that it escaped him. When the lion returned to eat the hare, he found that it had been awakened by the noise and had escaped.
   This story was told to make the point that men often lose moderate gains by trying for

   A. easier ones   B. larger ones
   C. sure profit   D. great losses

   3._____

4. In Norse mythology, no god was better loved than Balder, the god of light and peace. He was slain by the trickery of Loki, a jealous god.
   When the dark winter comes to the Norseland, the people say, "All nature grieves for Balder," and when the spring comes again, they say,

   A. "Summer is here again."
   B. "Balder has never lived."
   C. "Loki will never return to earth."
   D. "The spirit of Balder has returned."

   4._____

5. Living organisms are able to exist at great ocean depths in spite of the tremendous pressure of the water so long as their, body spaces are not filled with air or any other gas. This is possible because the pressure is equally applied on all sides of the organism and the same pressure is maintained inside and outside. Similarly, man does not feel the effects of pressure in the atmosphere exerted on him at 14.7 pounds per square inch, but he cannot withstand the great pressure of water below depths of 100 feet because his body contains spaces filled with _____ pressure.

   A. water at low
   B. air at the same
   C. water at high
   D. air at low

6. The oak tree has long been a symbol of strength and bravery. Mindful of this symbolism, the Romans, who were a hardy people, decorated their war heroes with crowns of _____ leaves.

   A. maple   B. olive   C. laurel   D. oak

7. In aviation, the ceiling is the distance from the ground to the bottom of the clouds when the sky is more than half-covered. When there is heavy fog on the ground, the ceiling is said to be zero. When the sky is clear or there are only scattered clouds, the ceiling is unlimited. An airplane pilot must know what the ceiling is before takeoff so that he can determine the proper flight

   A. altitude   B. direction   C. instruments   D. speed

8. In THE RIGHTS OF MAN, Thomas Paine wrote, *"Every age and generation must be as free to act for itself in all oases as the ages and generations which preceded it. The vanity and presumption of governing beyond the grave is the most ridiculous and insolent of ail tyrannies. Man has no property in man; neither has any generation a property in the generations which are to follow."*
   According to this, citizens of the United States should respect the Constitution because they believe it is right and not because it is

   A. debatable   B. old   C. English   D. misunderstood

9. Before newspapers were common, a man called a town crier was appointed to make public announcements. The town crier was an important person in England and in the British North American colonies, but he disappeared when newspapers became more widely distributed. Nowadays we often hear news before we read it in the paper. We hear it from an electronic town crier -

   A. the theater
   B. a radio or a television set
   C. a town meeting
   D. a phonograph

10. The opal is a gem that reflects a number of beautiful colors. For a long time, opals were unpopular because of a superstition that it was bad luck to wear them unless they were one's birthstone.
    Few people believe this superstition anymore, and opals have become more

    A. transparent   B. colorful   C. popular   D. beautiful

11. Newton's third law of motion states that for every action there is an equal and opposite reaction. When a gun is fired, the force that pushes the bullet forward is equal to the force with which the gun recoils.
Space vehicles, having left the earth's atmosphere, can maneuver by firing small rockets in the direction

    A. of the earth
    B. in which they wish to go
    C. opposite to their destination
    D. at right angles to their destination

12. When the purchasing power of the dollar steadily declines over a period of time, we speak of *inflation*. The reverse situation, in which a dollar buys more than formerly, is called deflation.
Inflation and deflation, then, are defined by changes in the relation between

    A. borrowing and lending
    B. money and goods
    C. supply and demand
    D. decrease and increase

13. The seed gatherers were a group of Indians who lived in the arid region between the Rocky Mountains and the Sierra Nevada. They were called seed gatherers because of the way in which they got most of their food. Seeds and berries suitable to eat grew in different regions at different times of the year.
For this reason, the seed gatherers

    A. were skilled archers
    B. changed homes often
    C. fished in the sea
    D. made fancy baskets

14. The men of the Coast Guard rescue many people from disasters at sea. Their work is often dangerous because they sometimes have to go out on a rescue mission under very bad conditions.
The men have excellent equipment, and they are well-trained, but their duties involve great

    A. speed   B. preparation   C. risks   D. thrills

15. A crocodile can snap a wooden plank in two with its powerful jaws. But a man can hold the jaws of a crocodile together with very little effort.
The crocodile exerts the greatest amount of power when

    A. snapping at wood
    B. opening its mouth
    C. C. lashing its tail
    D. closing its jaws

16. All of Alaska is farther west than the westernmost part of the continental United States. Juneau, the capital of Alaska, is in the same time zone as California, although its longitude should place it in the Yukon time zone. Some of the Aleutian Islands, a part of Alaska, are on one side of the 180 meridian and some are on the other, but the date line does not follow the 180 meridian and does not cut the Aleutians.
The result is that although there are four time zones in the United States, they are all

    A. on the same side of the date line
    B. on standard time
    C. really west of Greenwich
    D. in the Western Hemisphere

17. In Greek mythology, a chimera was a fire-breathing female monster with the head of a lion, the body of a goat, and the tail of a dragon. Of course, there really was no such animal, but the idea was so fantastic that we use the name chimera now for any

    A. deliberate falsehood
    B. figment of the imagination
    C. strange animal
    D. hybrid animal

18. The German shepherd is intelligent, alert, loyal, highly trainable, and has a good disposition. It is frequently used as a guide dog for the blind.
    It is sometimes called *German police dog* because so many of this breed have been trained for

    A. seeing eye dogs   B. police work
    C. army scouts   D. rescue work

19. Unless an adequate supply of protein is included in a person's diet, loss of weight and even death may result. The problem of determining the amount of protein needed is important in rationing food in war or in famine. The minimal requirement of protein to maintain the body in health is less when the protein consumed is animal protein than when it is vegetable protein.
    In some parts of the world, protein deficiency is a problem because the diet of the people is almost completely made up of

    A. animal proteins   B. fish
    C. solids   D. cereals

20. Emerson said, *"Character is adroitness to keep the old and trodden 'round, and power and courage to make new roads to new and better goals."*
    This means that the person of high character is both

    A. conformist and creator   B. friendly and aloof
    C. student and laborer   D. popular and unpopular

KEY (CORRECT ANSWERS)

1.	A	11.	C
2.	D	12.	B
3.	B	13.	B
4.	D	14.	C
5.	D	15.	D
6.	D	16.	A
7.	A	17.	B
8.	B	18.	B
9.	B	19.	D
10.	C	20.	A

TEST 2

DIRECTIONS: Each question or incomplete statement is followed by several suggested answers or completions. Select the one that BEST answers the question or completes the statement. *PRINT THE LETTER OF THE CORRECT ANSWER IN THE SPACE AT THE RIGHT.*

1. The small Boston terrier has a dark coat with white chest, neck, and feet. Many people are drawn to this dog because of its neat appearance and large brown eyes. The Boston terrier is a popular pet because it likes people and 1.____

    A. grows so large
    B. bites postmen
    C. is hard to train
    D. makes friends easily

2. The gradations of the moral faculties in the higher animals and man are so imperceptible that to deny to the first a certain sense of responsibility and consciousness would certainly be an exaggeration of the difference between animals and man.
   When animals fight with one another, when they associate for a common purpose, when they warn one another of danger, when they come to the rescue of another, when they display pain and joy, they manifest impulses of the same kind as are considered among the 2.____

    A. most general in the animal kingdom
    B. animal instincts of man
    C. divine provisions for man
    D. moral attributes of man

3. In ancient times, a country guaranteed its treaty promises by giving hostages to the other party. The hostages were often important people in their own country. They were held as prisoners and could be killed if their country failed to keep its treaty promises.
   Today, most countries rely on the good faith of other countries and on public opinion to ensure that they will keep their treaties, and the hostage system 3.____

    A. is strictly observed
    B. is no longer used
    C. protects treaty makers
    D. has grown in effectiveness

4. The Pekingese was held in great esteem by Chinese royalty. The dog was bred to accentuate marks that were related in various ways to the upper classes of society. A white spot on the forehead of a Pekingese was admired, for this mark was associated with the Buddha.
   A mark round the dog's body resembling a sash was quite admirable, for during the time when the Pekingese breed was so much admired, 4.____

    A. sashes were used to hold the outer garments together
    B. only high-ranking officials could wear sashes
    C. it was difficult to breed a dog with a sash mark
    D. sash marks signified royal blood

5. A recent U.S. study showed that of 100 high school seniors who received national academic scholarships, nine out of ten read at least one book a month, while of 100 high school seniors accepted by various colleges but not awarded scholarships, only six out of ten read at least one book a month.
   This shows that those who read more are MOST likely to

   A. waste time
   B. achieve more
   C. become librarians
   D. spend less money

6. Turbines in motor vehicles cannot be operated on gasoline containing lead. Diesel fuel, on which turbines can be operated, is available only on major turnpikes and on roads that trucks use.
   Thus, if regular cars are to utilize turbines,

   A. highways must be rerouted
   B. the turbines must be small
   C. diesel fuel distribution must be expanded
   D. filling stations must stop selling regular gasoline

7. A gun collector of my acquaintance owns an old rifle that sold for about $35 twenty years ago and would now bring a price of $400 to $450. But it isn't always easy to make money on antiques. Experts warn that people who have never dabbled in antiques should study the market carefully, choose a few specialties, read every available book in those fields, and consult reliable dealers before buying. They say that few pieces will be acquired cheaply by the

   A. inexperienced seller
   B. gun collector
   C. novice collector
   D. country tourist

8. Dinosaurs were the largest land animals ever known. They were sixty to ninety feet long. These figures are not guesses; they are based on measurements of bones that have been

   A. found   B. painted   C. reproduced   D. molded

9. Painting goes back at least as far as the time of cavemen. Wall paintings have been found inside some of their caves. It is believed that these pictures were not drawn primarily for decoration because most of them are

   A. pictures of animals rather than of people
   B. far back in the cave away from all light
   C. unrelated to the cavemen's lives
   D. intricate drawings that have beauty

10. The ermine, a native of northern countries, is a weasel with valuable fur. In the summer the fur is brown, but as the weather gets cooler, the fur gets lighter until it is pure white during the coldest part of the year. Since most people prefer the white ermine pelts, most ermine trapping is done

    A. with specialized traps
    B. in early fall
    C. after the snow disappears
    D. during the winter

11. The pilot of an airplane is dependent upon the plane's radio for communication from the ground concerning takeoff, landing, the movements of other planes, and the weather. The safety of the passengers in the plane is dependent upon this communication. In case the radio is out of order, a pilot may use other signals, such as lights, but the radio is very important.
    Even small planes are usually equipped with.

    A. radios   B. landing gear   C. horns   D. pilots

12. Although more men than women play golf, women have played the game for many years. Mary, Queen of Scots, who lived in the sixteenth century, may have been the first woman golfer. She used the term *cadet* (pupil) for the boy who carried her clubs around the course.
    This term is still used today, but the spelling has been changed to

    A. Scotsman   B. cadet   C. caddy   D. golfer

13. According to Emerson, "A man is a center for nature, running out threads of relation through everything, fluid and solid, material and elemental... How few materials are yet used by our arts! It would seem as if each waited like the enchanted princes in fairy tales, for a destined human deliverer. All that is yet inanimate will one day speak and reason. Unpublished nature will have its whole secret told."
    If Emerson were to come to life in the twentieth century, he would

    A. lose his faith in fairy tales
    B. not be surprised by man's advancement in outer space
    C. feel compelled to use more materials in his arts
    D. be frightened by this industrial age

14. At one time, California had to ship its products around Cape Horn, which is at the southern tip of South America, to get them to the eastern part of the United States. This route was long, but the land routes were worse because of the mountains, deserts, and plains. It is not surprising that California planned a big celebration in 1914 to emphasize the importance of the opening of

    A. the Panama Canal   B. eastern harbors
    C. European routes   D. Chinese trade

15. Gordius, mythical king of Phrygia, tied an intricate knot in the thong that held the pole of his chariot to the yoke. An oracle had declared that he who untied the knot should be master of Asia. Many tried and failed. Alexander the Great looked at the knot and quickly cut it with his sword. We use the expression *to cut the Gordian knot* to mean to

    A. do the impossible
    B. use your head instead of your hands
    C. solve a difficult problem by bold action
    D. become an oracle

16. Many millions of dollars worth of gold, silver, and jewels have gone down with ships in numerous ship disasters. These treasures lie at the bottom of almost every major body of water in the world.
    It is not surprising that divers spend a great deal of time and money looking for

    A. treasure islands   B. sunken treasure
    C. scientific data   D. new oceans

17. The following quotation is from Thomas Hobbes: *"Nature has made men so equal in the faculties of body and mind* as that though there be found one man sometimes manifestly stronger in body, or of quicker mind than another, yet when all is reckoned together, the difference between man and man is not so considerable as that one man can thereupon claim to himself any benefit to which another

    A. has already attained."
    B. is capable of attaining."
    C. may not reach as well as he."
    D. would deny him."

18. The Louvre in Paris has the restoration of a stone found in 1868 at Dhiban in what was ancient Moab. The stone is believed to have been carved by a scribe about 800 B.C. and is of interest to scholars of ancient languages. When the French tried to buy the stone, the Arabs broke it into many pieces, hoping to get more money for it.
    The French bought some of the larger pieces and were able to make the restoration of the entire stone because a French embassy official at Constantinople (now Istanbul) had

    A. made a paper cast of the stone
    B. hidden the original from the Turks
    C. had the writing deciphered
    D. handled the financial arrangements

19. There are many primitive countries in the world that have never taken a census, an official count of the population. Population figures from these countries are

    A. accurate   B. too high   C. estimates   D. lost

20. The National Audubon Society reported that their 1962 census of bald eagles in the United States, excluding Alaska, was 3807, as compared to 3642 in 1961. Of 118 dead eagles reported to the society in 1962, 91 had been shot. There is great concern that the bald eagle, which is the national bird, may completely disappear.
    The Audubon Society urges a nationwide campaign to educate the public not to _____ eagles.

    A. protect   B. feed   C. harm   D. count

KEY (CORRECT ANSWERS)

1.	D	11.	A
2.	D	12.	C
3.	B	13.	B
4.	B	14.	A
5.	B	15.	C
6.	C	16.	B
7.	C	17.	C
8.	A	18.	A
9.	B	19.	C
10.	D	20.	C

TEST 3

DIRECTIONS: Each question or incomplete statement is followed by several suggested answers or completions. Select the one that BEST answers the question or completes the statement. *PRINT THE LETTER OF THE CORRECT ANSWER IN THE SPACE AT THE RIGHT.*

1. A library may be very large, but if it is in disorder, it is not as useful as one that is small but

    A. disordered
    B. closed to the public
    C. nearby
    D. well arranged

    1._____

2. It is no great wonder if in the long process of time, while fortune takes her course hither and thither, numerous coincidences should spontaneously occur.
   If the number of subjects to be wrought upon be infinite, it is all the more easy for fortune, with such an abundance of material, to

    A. effect this similarity of results
    B. fill all men with wonder
    C. prevent spontaneous coincidences
    D. effect a man's success

    2._____

3. Clearinghouses are useful in reducing the volume of concrete interbank transactions. Each member bank sends to the clearinghouse a record of the money it has paid out on checks drawn on each other member.
   When the lists are compared, equal reciprocal debts are

    A. reduced   B. collected   C. recorded   D. canceled

    3._____

4. Many citizens of other nations deposit their money in banks in Switzerland. The Swiss banks carefully protect the identities of their depositors, a matter of some importance to certain depositors. An agent trying to determine if someone has money in a particular Swiss bank sometimes tries to make a deposit in the name of that person.
   Since the acceptance of such a deposit would imply that the account did exist, Swiss banks will not

    A. cash large checks for depositors
    B. accept deposits that have been mailed in
    C. allow foreigners to open checking accounts
    D. accept deposits from unidentified persons

    4._____

5. Very few states have done anything to ensure that untrained people are not allowed to carry guns. Safe gun loading can be taught, and if people had to pass a test before they could obtain a hunting license, the number of shooting accidents would probably

    A. pass laws   B. fail   C. increase   D. decrease

    5._____

6. In a Dutch auction, so called because it originated in the Netherlands, the auctioneer offers an object for sale at a price above its value. He gradually reduces the price until someone accepts it. In a regular auction, the auctioneer asks for an opening bid, which is always low. Then the auctioneer tries to get people to make higher bids and sells when no one will raise the bid.
   These two methods, though opposite in procedure, may both reach a sale at the highest price

    A. anyone is willing to pay
    B. that is fair to the buyer
    C. that the object is worth
    D. the seller can demand

    6._____

99

7. Optical glass is used in cameras, telescopes, eyeglasses, and many kinds of scientific equipment. The glass is almost flawless; it must be made with great care and only from the finest materials.
For these reasons, optical glass is

   A. expensive   B. scientific   C. brittle   D. unavailable

8. It was quite understandable that it was the policy of the old priest-nobles of Egypt and India to divert their peoples from becoming familiar with the seas and to represent the occupation of a seaman as incompatible with the purity of the highest caste.
The sea deserved to be hated by those who wished to maintain the old aristocracies, inasmuch as

   A. the sea has been the mightiest instrument in the leveling of mankind
   B. the life of a sailor was quite dangerous
   C. many of the sailors lost their lives while on voyages
   D. the priest-nobles were trying to further the spread of education

9. Six cities of ancient Palestine were set aside as places of refuge for people who had killed any person unawares. In these cities, the accused could receive a fair trial. If he was found guilty of intentional murder, he was returned for punishment to the place from which he had escaped.
But if the killing was found to be accidental or not willful, the accused was allowed to remain safely in

   A. his boyhood home   B. a country of exile
   C. the city of refuge   D. the original prison

10. The average density of a cubic foot of earth is about 5.5 times that of a cubic foot of water. This is determined by dividing the earth mass by its volume. However, rocks on the earth's surface have an average density of approximately 2.7.
Therefore, in order to offset the lighter weight of the surface materials, the interior of the earth MUST have a density

   A. of 5.5   B. greater than 5.5
   C. less than 5.5   D. less than 2.7

11. Our opinions and actions are influenced to a great extent by words - the words we read and the words we hear. Yet we do not carefully attend to the subtle implications, good or bad, conveyed by these words through association.
Some words are slippery: they gloss over the actual attributes of the thing to which they refer. For example, the supporters of a favored point of view are *progressive* while those who hold an opinion less to our liking are *radical*.
The words that are chosen imply

   A. only one interpretation   B. precisely what they state
   C. no subtle connotation   D. more than they state

12. When the Mormons who settled in the Valley of the Great Salt Lake applied for statehood in 1849, they wanted the name of the state to be Deseret. Deseret is the Mormon word for honeybee, which the Mormons had taken as a symbol of the work they all had to do to make the desert productive. They were refused statehood and remained the Territory of Utah until 1896, when Utah became the forty-fifth state. The state seal has a beehive on it, and the official motto of the state is *Industry.* These are tributes to Utah's

    A. acceptance as a state
    B. principal occupation
    C. Ute Indians
    D. early Mormon settlers

    12._____

13. Pythagoras, an ancient Greek, discovered the true nature of the harmonic series by observing the vibration of a single taut string stretched over a resonator. When a movable bridge was placed at the string's midpoint, the string vibrated in two segments at twice the speed at which it vibrated without a bridge. When moved to a third of the string's length, the string would vibrate in three segments at three times the speed. This phenomenon was repeated with each successive position of the bridge. Thus, Pythagoras was able to express the pitch relationships of the harmonic series in terms of

    A. mathematical ratios
    B. string lengths
    C. musical notation
    D. chemical formulas

    13._____

14. Not only were the Romans undemocratic, but at no period of its history did Rome love equality. In the Republic, rank was determined by wealth. The census was the basis of the social system. Every citizen had to declare his fortune before a magistrate, and his grade was then assigned him.
    Poverty and wealth established the

    A. legal differences between men
    B. democratic system of the Republic
    C. need for a strong judicial system
    D. social equality among men

    14._____

15. A surveyor's chain has 100 links, each 792 inches long. The chain is a unit of measurement that for most purposes would be very awkward, but it is particularly useful in surveying land because ten square chains made on acre. The original measuring instrument was actually made of chains. A surveyor's chain has 100 links, each 792 inches long. The chain is a unit of measurement that for most purposes would be very awkward, but it is particularly useful in surveying land because ten square chains made on acre.
    The original measuring instrument was actually made of chains.

    A. numerical   B. accurate   C. awkward   D. easy

    15._____

16. Millions of people in the world spend as much as one-third of their days by hauling water. Their diets are determined by a water shortage that restricts the variety of their agricultural products.
    If the scientists of the United States can increase the water supply of arid regions by removing the salt from sea-water, they will gain

    A. new travel opportunities abroad
    B. new export articles
    C. the gratitude of millions
    D. great profits from friends

    16._____

17. *"A friend stands at the door,
In either tight-closed hand
Hiding rich gifts, three hundred
And three score."*
These lines are from a poem titled

   A. EASTER MORNING B. CHRISTMAS EVE
   C. NEW YEAR'S EVE D. THANKSGIVING DAY

18. Our repugnance to death increases in proportion to our consciousness of having lived in vain - to the

   A. usefulness of our lives
   B. keenness of our disappointments
   C. intensity of our physical suffering
   D. greatness of our vanity

19. The ripeness or unripeness of the occasion must ever be well weighed; and generally it is good to commit the beginnings of all great actions to Argus with his hundred eyes, and the ends to Briareus with his hundred hands; first to watch, and then to

   A. consider   B. decide   C. begin   D. speed

20. Benjamin Franklin said, *"We may perhaps learn to deprive large masses of their Gravity, and give them absolute Levity for the sake of easy Transport. Agriculture may diminish its Labour and double its Produce; all Diseases may by sure means be prevented or cured, not excepting even that of old Age, and our Lives lengthened at pleasure even beyond the antediluvian Standard. O that moral science were in as fair a way of*

   A. Acceptance   B. Cure   C. Religion   D. Study

KEY (CORRECT ANSWERS)

1.	D	11.	D
2.	A	12.	D
3.	D	13.	A
4.	D	14.	A
5.	D	15.	D
6.	A	16.	C
7.	A	17.	C
8.	C	18.	B
9.	C	19.	D
10.	B	20.	D

www.ingramcontent.com/pod-product-compliance
Lightning Source LLC
Chambersburg PA
CBHW082126230426
43671CB00015B/2824